Caught Up

GENDER AND JUSTICE

Edited by Claire M. Renzetti

This University of California Press series explores how the experiences of offending, victimization, and justice are profoundly influenced by the intersections of gender with other markers of social location. Cross-cultural and comparative, series volumes publish the best new scholarship that seeks to challenge assumptions, highlight inequalities, and transform practice and policy.

Caught Up

Girls, Surveillance, and
Wraparound Incarceration

JERRY FLORES

UNIVERSITY OF CALIFORNIA PRESS

University of California Press, one of the most
distinguished university presses in the United
States, enriches lives around the world by
advancing scholarship in the humanities, social
sciences, and natural sciences. Its activities are
supported by the UC Press Foundation and by
philanthropic contributions from individuals
and institutions. For more information, visit
www.ucpress.edu.

University of California Press
Oakland, California

© 2016 by The Regents of the University of California

Library of Congress Cataloging-in-Publication Data

Names: Flores, Jerry, 1985- author.
Title: Caught up : girls, surveillance, and
    wraparound incarceration / Jerry Flores.
Description: Oakland, California : University of
    California Press, [2016] | Includes bibliographical
    references and index.
Identifiers: LCCN 2016023976 (print) | LCCN
    2016026487 (ebook) | ISBN 9780520284876 (cloth :
    alk. paper) | ISBN 9780520284883 (pbk. : alk.
    paper) | ISBN 9780520960541 (e-edition)
Subjects: LCSH: Female juvenile delinquents—
    California, Southern—Case studies. | Hispanic
    American teenage girls—Education (Secondary)—
    California, Southern—Case studies. | Hispanic
    American teenage girls—California, Southern—
    Social conditions—Case studies. | Juvenile
    detention homes—California, Southern—Case
    studies.
Classification: LCC HV6046 .F55 2016 (print) | LCC
    HV6046 (ebook) | DDC 364.36092/527949—dc23
LC record available at https://lccn.loc
    .gov/2016023976

25 24 23 22 21 20 19 18 17 16
10 9 8 7 6 5 4 3 2 1

CONTENTS
_____

ACKNOWLEDGMENTS

I am grateful and indebted to a large number of people for their continued guidance and support over the last six years. I thank my mentors Nikki Jones, Denise Segura, Victor Rios, John Sutton, and Kyra Greene. Each of you showed me a unique and dynamic way to mentor students; this mentorship allowed me to forge my own academic career. You also taught me to be a kind and reflexive human being who puts social justice at the center of my personal and professional work. I now use these skills as a faculty member, researcher, and mentor. I also thank the following institutions and organizations: Options for Youth, Grossmont College, Pasadena City College, San Diego State University, and University of California, Santa Barbara. Countless faculty and staff members in these organizations shaped my professional pathway, and I am forever grateful. I thank, too, the Ford Foundation, the University of California President's Postdoctoral Fellowship, the Chicano Studies Institute (UC Santa Barbara), and the Social Work and Criminal Justice Program at the University of Washington Tacoma for providing me with generous economic support for this project.

I also thank my colleagues at University of Washington Tacoma for their continued support and inspiration. A special thanks to Janelle Eliasson Nannini, Eric Madfis, Alissa Ackerman, and Jeff Cohen. Your support and comments helped improve the manuscript, and your friendship is priceless. A special thanks as well to my dearest friends and colleagues, O. G. Xuan Santos and Gustavo Barahona-Lopez. Xuan, you are the older brother I always wanted; and, Gustavo, you are the friend I always needed. My family and I are blessed to have you both in our lives. I also thank Amada Armenta: without your help all those years ago I would not have made it into graduate school, and I would not have completed this manuscript or my PhD. I thank, too, the reviewers at the University of California Press for their insightful comments and critiques. They helped improve the manuscript in immeasurable ways.

I offer a very special thanks to my wife and partner, Angie Henao. Thank you for being so amazing and supportive. I appreciate your encouragement and your willingness to hear all my ideas and presentations (and jokes) before they ever see a classroom or conference. You are the best thing that every happened to me, and I am grateful to have you in my life. And I thank my son, Sol Gael Henao Flores. I named you after the book *Soledad Brother* by George Jackson. This book inspired me, and I know one day it will do the same for you. I hope that in the future you will become as proud of me as I am of you. I also thank my parents, Carmen Flores and Gerardo M. Flores, for their hard work, years of dedication, and willingness to leave their lives in Mexico to find better opportunities for their children in the United States. Along these same lines, I thank my brothers, David Flores and Esau Flores. Both of you are amazing people, and you are doing great things for our community. You two provide me with more hope and encouragement than you can imagine.

Finally, I thank all the young women in my study. Thank you for sharing your daily struggles and victories. I hope this book has a positive effect on your lives and the lives of other young people like you. I also thank all the professionals (especially Ms. Sanchez) who helped facilitate this study. Although I critique the criminal justice and educational systems, there are still kind and compassionate people in it who try to improve young people's lives. I hope my work does not overshadow your efforts.

As I have said in the past, I believe we can live in a society where prisons and detention centers of all kinds are no longer necessary. A world where the criminal justice and educational systems can become institutions for social change, instead of organizations that discipline and punish individuals. I can imagine a future where we help transform people who have committed mistakes in ways that do not require a carceral experience. I firmly believe we are slowly working toward that reality, and I hope this book helps achieve this goal.

Introduction

I leave my house at about seven in the morning on a typical sunshine-filled day in Southern California. Out my car window, the Pacific Ocean glistens with seemingly endless rays of sun. Near the end of my forty-mile trip this morning, a new-model black truck holds up traffic in the fast lane. While I'm still trying to maneuver around it, I notice my exit is a mile and a half away. After successfully crossing three lanes of traffic to make it to the far-right lane, I pick up my camera in hopes of taking a picture of the freeway sign for the juvenile detention center, which is posted at the side of the road. A later glimpse at my camera while I wait for a red light shows me that I missed the first sign as well as the second: the frame shows only branches and sky.

After a right at the exit, I drive through a neighborhood that looks a lot like the working-class Latino enclave where I grew up. This area has a dingy, worn-down look: The paint on the buildings is faded, cracked, and peeling. The storefronts have signs in Spanish: "barato" (cheap) and "oferta" (sale). On my right, I see a sheetrock shop followed by a few liquor stores, a small used car lot, a strip mall with a donut shop, a cell phone store, and a discount shoe outlet; on my left, a gas station and a *carniceria* (Mexican butcher shop). It's a struggle to keep my eyes on the road. A bit farther along, the storefronts give way to farmland. A seemingly random public school appears after about another half a mile. Despite the lack of razor wire, it looks remarkably like a detention facility, complete with steel-colored roofs, tan paint, basketball courts, and two pristine baseball diamonds. A huge crater about a hundred feet deep and three hundred feet wide sits right next to the school, looking like an old mining site that no one bothered to cover or fill. Before reaching the detention center, I pass a few peach-colored self-storage buildings and two lonely fruit stands. On my left, the sky-blue background and stainless-steel lettering of the sign for the detention facility catch my eyes. I again try to take a picture, but this time my camera refuses to turn on.

I drive straight ahead and encounter another sign in the same style but with different text. One arrow, pointing straight ahead, signals the way to the "Juvenile facilities." A second, pointing to the right, indicates the "Juvenile courthouse." A third arrow, pointing to the left, reads, "Freight deliveries." The last arrow, pointing to the right, reads, "Booking." I turn right and park in front of the detention center.

Visitors exiting their cars and approaching the facility first encounter a few tan-colored concrete benches attached to the sidewalk. A dozen red, white, pink, and yellow rose bushes dot the green lawn. The facility itself is painted various colors. The exterior of the detention facility has the same checkered tile pattern as the courthouse. The detention facility, however, looks newer and has only one story. A piece of the facility sticks out in front of the entrance like a perpendicular flying buttress. Apprehensive about what comes next, I stay in my car for a few minutes. A sign on the front of the building with the same sky-blue background and steel letters as the one at the entrance reads, "El Valle Juvenile Detention Facility."[1]

To the right of the entrance stands a large gray fence about twenty feet high, the top of which curls inward, toward the facility, making it difficult for individuals inside to climb this edifice. A second, parallel fence beyond this one gives away the building's purpose as a detention facility. Minus the well-hidden fence, which cannot be seen from the street, the facility looks like a school or a suite of office buildings; the whole detention-center complex looks as if it is disguised as a courthouse. If you were to stand in front of the facility and turn 180 degrees, you would see a large expanse of farmland and a four-lane road. I move my car in search of a better view through the tall fence, but its bottom portion is obscured by a tarp or some other, wooden structure. I repark my car and wait.

A few people walk into the facility, including an odd-looking trio. The first person to enter is a white man about sixty-five years old. The hair on both his head and his arms is predominantly gray, and both his head and his arms feature deep wrinkles. His white shirt is tucked into faded blue jeans; his stomach hangs below his waist and obscures his belt. He is accompanied by a bald, light-skinned Latino man about six feet tall who looks to be about twenty-nine years old. The younger man is clean-shaven and wears a loose-fitting white shirt, khaki shorts that reach below the middle of his shin, and white tennis shoes and socks. His long socks are pulled up past the end of his shorts so that no part of his leg is uncovered. A white woman who looks about thirty years old walks between them. She wears a baggy blue hoodie and faded black jeans. Her dark brown hair is wound into curls so stiff from hair spray that they look like they might break. Her hair and makeup, which she has clearly spent a lot of time preparing, contrast with her dingy clothes and shoes and the way she holds her shoulders and head. I can see crow's feet beginning to form around her eyes, which makes me believe that she has aged superficially. The two men talk to each other while the woman, silently walking between the two males, looks at the ground.

In the parking lot, another individual sits in his car. He is short, with dark hair and dark auburn skin. He reminds me of my father's side of the family, which looks more indigenous than European. I am parked behind him; he looks at me through his rearview mirror. His keeps his facial expression blank and looks away as soon as I look up. When the parking lot clears, I notice the American and California flags on the front of the facility. Meanwhile, another woman has left the facility. She looks Latina and pulls a name tag off her bright yellow shirt while she walks to her car. She, too, wears a blank expression.

At 8:30 A.M. I walk into the building. Before entering, I stop to take a picture of a set of rules, posted in English and Spanish, with my cell phone. This time, I have no opportunity to check to see how the picture came out. I open one of two double doors and walk straight ahead. In front of me, a light green steel frame holds tinted windows in place, replicating a similar structure outside. To my right is a gray cinder-block wall. The floor has large white tiles with narrow strips of dark gray mortar running between them. To my left, I see a small desk with a slender gray metal detector beside it.

Stationed there is a portly Latino man dressed in a brown deputy suit. He makes eye contact with me but says nothing. I notice some kind of a badge on his lapel as he motions me forward with his hand. I step through the metal detector, and he signals me through to the waiting area. The room is brightly lit; it feels like a hospital, sterile and cold. In front of me, I see a row of six white steel chairs. Another row of four chairs is pushed against the wall to the left, one of them supporting a flat-screen television. A formal reception area enclosed by three large windows is located to the right. The glass is thick, with thin, crisscrossing wires embedded throughout.

A petite Filipino woman about fifty years old comes to greet me through a two-way speaker on the other side of the glass. She has to hunch down to speak into the microphone. When I tell her I am here with the "school," her intense look softens. She smiles, and she asks me to sit down. As I sit there taking notes, a thirty-year-old Latina comes through a large steel door located to the left of the reception area and asks, "Are you Jerry?" I tell her I am. She shakes my hand and asks me to follow her into the facility. We walk to the large steel door, and she pushes a small steel button on the door, which buzzes and clicks. She proceeds to open the door.

As we walk through the entryway, the space opens up; it seems brighter. To the right, there are several isolation cells. They are used for holding people who are being transferred to other parts of the jail or to other detention centers. To my left is the jail's central control unit, inside of which are two officers in charge of opening and closing the detention center doors. A large tinted window separates the control unit from the detention center. Directly in front of us is a large steel-and-glass door that separates the control unit from the main jail. The entryway to the latter is the largest I have seen entering the facility. A law enforcement badge is emblazed on its surface. The woman and I both wave hello to the officers, and they let us enter.

As we continue walking through the facility, I notice that the wall to my right is made of cinder block; the one on my left is made of a green metal mesh. Through it, I can see a set of basketball courts and a small soccer field in the middle of the facility. After about ten minutes, we arrive at a building that houses the units where the youth in this facility live. We walk down a long corridor—cinder block on both sides—for several seconds before arriving at another steel door, to our right. The woman escorting me hits the steel button located on this door, and a buzz-and-click sequence is initiated once again. She waits for me to walk through the door and then waves good-bye.

Unlike the corridor we were just in, this space is meant to hold youth throughout their time in detention. This room is about twenty feet tall and seventy feet long and has a ground floor as well as an upper level that you can see from where I stand. Directly in front of me, I see some sunlight. That light is coming from an exercise yard about fifteen feet square. Three of the room's walls are made of gray cinder blocks, and the remaining one is made of thick glass held in place by a gray steel frame. A door in the right-hand corner of this glass wall leads to the exercise yard. And to the right of that door, a platform about three feet off the ground holds four computers and a microphone. This area serves as the control center for the unit. The two correctional officers sitting there look over at me with indifference, then turn back to their computers. They are both Latina, slender, with dark hair, and are wearing blue jeans and dark shirts. They are also wearing utility belts with handcuffs, pepper spray, and a baton. To my left, I see a steel table with six benches attached. Further left, I see two floors of cells, with four cells on each floor. To the far right, a concrete staircase with a steel railing leads to the second floor.

As I step forward and turn farther to the right, almost behind me appears the open door to a classroom full of students, along with a teacher and a correctional guard. I begin to walk toward the classroom. On my way there, I notice a girl who looks familiar sitting at one of the multiple stainless-steel tables located in this common area known as the "day room." I recognize Flor, a sixteen-year-old Latina whom I know has a two-year-old daughter, from my previous visits to El Valle.[2] She has short, coarse hair. She greets me with a somber, "Hey." I ask her how she's doing. Her eyes are puffy, and I can tell that she's been crying. She says, "I was so good for three months. I was doing so good. But I tested dirty on Friday. I tried to wash it out but—it stays with you for a long time. They tested me on Friday and I got here yesterday. I feel so bad. . . . And today is my Mom's birthday, and I don't even have her number." As she begins to cry, I ask, "Where did they test you? Who tested you?" She replies, "Probation. At Legacy. I will never get off probation. . . . I was there for three months, and I am back here. Fuck!"

Flor describes a predicament common to the approximately twenty-three thousand students who attend one of the 283 California Community Day Schools (California Department of Education, 2010). "Legacy" is Legacy Community Day School.[3] Community day schools serve expelled students,

students with few high school credits, students referred by school attendance review boards, and other high-risk youths (California Department of Education, 2012a). Students at these schools encounter low student-teacher ratios, but they also come in contact with school counselors, psychologists, academic and vocational counselors, law enforcement officers, probation officers, and human services agency personnel. At Legacy, youth are routinely searched, drug-tested at will, and arrested.

Between September 2009 and October 2011, I conducted ethnographic research at these two sites, getting to know the lives of the girls who shuttled between the school and the detention center. In what follows, I have used this research to document the changing nature of discipline and education in the era of mass incarceration. Since almost all the young women in my study were Latina, I've used my findings to explore the gendered, racialized, and socioeconomic nuances of Latina girls' experiences and their paths in and out of secure detention.

In recent years, criminology, sociology, and education scholars have paid more attention to the connection between schools and institutions of confinement (Winn, 2011; Winn, 2010; Kim, Losen, and Hewitt, 2010; Morris, 2007; Chesney-Lind and Jones, 2010; Chesney-Lind and Shelden, 2004). Most research in this area focuses on youths' experiences in schools and their increased exposure to surveillance in this setting (Winn, 2011; Winn, 2010; Díaz-Cotto, 2006; González-López, 2006; Simkins et al., 2004). So far, little work has investigated how young people's pathways to deviance are shaped by the increasing material and economic ties between schools and the criminal justice system. And even fewer works address the unique experiences of the growing numbers of young Latinas who are navigating these multiple institutions. In this book I have used ethnographic research to analyze how these education and penal institutions are materially, economically, and administratively connected.

My research was guided by several questions suggested by this literature. The first set of questions centers on understanding the girls' experiences. How do they first come in contact with the criminal justice system? How do they experience incarceration, and how do they eventually exit the criminal justice system? A second set of concerns asks how their treatment at home, school, detention, and Legacy creates the conditions that lead them back to El Valle

Juvenile Detention Facility. The third set of questions focuses specifically on the institutional links between these two supposedly different sorts of places. What is the relationship between El Valle Juvenile Detention Facility and Legacy Community School, and what are the consequences of this connection for Latina students? Finally, I explore how race, class, gender, and sexuality shape girls' experiences as they pass through these multiple institutions.

During the course of my fieldwork, I discovered a dynamic juncture between these two sites. In this connection, the probation department that controls El Valle has economically and administratively inserted itself into the everyday practices of Legacy School. This has resulted in young people in this community day school, and specifically in the recuperation program, being bounced back and forth between the two settings. This phenomenon is not uncommon for girls and boys in California; a number of scholars have projected that the percentage of students in these schools will continue to grow as California's public schools battle financial and academic pressures at every level of government (Malagon and Alvarez, 2010). Indeed, the connection between community day schools and detention centers that I analyze exists in almost every county in the state and disproportionately affects low-income Latina and Latino youth (Flores, 2012).

The connection between these sites is no accident. Rather, administrators at Legacy Community Day School and El Valle Juvenile Detention Facility have achieved a level of integration between their two facilities in an attempt to provide young people with so-called wraparound services. In theory, this well-intentioned idea provides youth with support from social service professionals at home, at school, and in the actual detention center. In practice, however, the results are less desirable. I argue that wraparound services more closely resemble a phenomenon I call *wraparound incarceration*,[4] where students cannot escape the surveillance associated with formal detention despite leaving the actual detention center. My project as a whole shows how young Latinas first end up behind bars, how they experience detention, and what their lives are like when they leave these detention facilities. I also show how their pathways through home, detention, and school are shaped by their race, class, gender, and sexuality. Finally, I identify some of the key turning points at which girls can extricate themselves from the criminal justice system.

GIRLS, CRIME, AND ABUSE IN THE HOME

Scholars have identified several home factors that determine whether girls step onto a path leading to the criminal justice system. Researchers overwhelmingly identify abuse in the home as a leading factor in determining whether girls tread pathways to future imprisonment (Winn, 2011; Winn, 2010; Díaz-Cotto, 2006; Simkins et al., 2004; Chesney-Lind and Shelden, 2004; Kakar, Friedemann, Peck, 2002; Schaffner, 1998). In a qualitative investigation based in Philadelphia, Simkins and colleagues found that previous abuse in the home is directly connected to maladjustment in school, drug use, and subsequent incarceration. For example, most girls who eventually are incarcerated "had at least one parent who abuses drugs and/or alcohol; [or they have] experienced some type of trauma (sexual or physical abuse, neglect or witnessed violence)" (Simkins et al., 2004, 59). This kind of abuse also includes psychological mistreatment. Girls experience sexual abuse more often in the home than do boys (Winn, 2011; Winn, 2010; Chesney-Lind and Shelden, 2004; Simkins et al., 2004; Kakar, Friedemann, Peck, 2002). Sexual abuse can lead to a host of physical and psychological issues and is linked to drug use and future victimization at the hands of strangers, acquaintances, or significant others (Winn, 2011; Chesney-Lind and Shelden, 2004; Schaffner, 1998).

Feminist criminologists explain that girls often run away to escape physical and sexual abuse in the home (Chesney-Lind and Jones, 2010; Chesney-Lind and Shelden, 2004; Schaffner, 1998). Girls leave their homes in higher numbers when they are victimized by family members (Chesney-Lind and Shelden, 2004). For example, in her qualitative study of previously incarcerated Latinas, Díaz-Cotto found that Latina women experienced incest more often than white and Black girls did (Díaz-Cotto, 2006; see also González-López, 2006). Ironically, girls are more likely than boys to fight back against abuse and more likely to attempt to run away from the abuse they are experiencing in their homes. Both of these actions frequently lead to police contact; in practice, this means that parents criminalize girls' survival strategies (Chesney-Lind, 2010; Chesney-Lind and Shelden, 2004). In this way, girls' experiences of abuse at home often lead to their first contact with the criminal justice system and their subsequent incarceration.

Other scholars have found that girls can be arrested at the request of their parents for being "incorrigible." This broad term usually refers to behaviors that violate idealized notions of femininity. These behaviors might include fighting back against abuse, sleeping "all day," not doing chores, challenging parents' authority, overtly expressing sexuality, deviating from heteronormativity, or running away from home (Winn, 2011; Winn, 2010; Sharma, 2010; Chesney-Lind and Shelden, 2004; Bettie, 2003). Although some of these actions do not specifically merit criminal punishment, parents can fabricate criminal behavior to have girls arrested for these seemingly trivial behaviors.

Girls who find themselves in this kind of home environment often, as already noted, choose to leave. Once they do so, the kinds of behaviors they engage in can lead directly to incarceration. For example, when girls run away from home, they often miss school (Díaz-Cotto, 2006; Casella, 2003), which can result in their being sent to group homes or continuation schools or directly to juvenile detention. Girls who run away are also more likely to use drugs and alcohol, which puts them at risk of arrest but also exposes them to further victimization (Simkins et al., 2004; Schaffner, 1998). Once intoxicated, youth are also more likely to have unprotected sex, consume more-addictive drugs, or participate in further criminal behavior (Winn, 2011; Díaz-Cotto, 2006; Bettie, 2003). Youth, moreover, often have to "hustle" to take care of themselves while living outside the home. For example, girls (and boys) may participate in survival sex, shoplift food and clothing, or work in other illicit trades to stay alive (Chesney-Lind and Shelden, 2004; Schaffner, 1998). In a quantitative study using a national data set, Park, Morash, and Stevens found that "early-age runaway girls (before twelve or thirteen) reported significantly more (249 percent more) . . . assaults than other girls" (2010, 320). Running away at an early age, then, exposes girls to multiple forms of risk, from physical assault to addiction to arrest.

Ultimately, girls' survival strategies on the street make them more vulnerable to arrest and other forms of victimization (Díaz-Cotto, 2006). Young women who run away from home tend to stay away for fear of more family abuse (Díaz-Cotto, 2006). The criminalization of girls' survival strategies has been a consistent finding in research on gender and crime for the last twenty years (Chesney-Lind and Jones, 2010; Chesney-Lind and Shelden, 2004; Chesney-Lind and Pasko, 2012; Chesney-Lind, 1986).

GENDER IN A TOTAL INSTITUTION

Like jails and prisons, juvenile detention centers are "total institutions." Erving Goffman describes a "total institution" as "a place of residence and work where a large number of like-situated individuals, cut off from the wider society for an appreciable period of time, together lead an enclosed, formally administered round of life" (1961, xiii). These institutions train inmates to accept notions of social control by stripping them of agency, autonomy, and self-identity. Goffman explains, for example, how detention centers re-create power hierarchies to ensure that inmates will play the role of "captive" with little resistance.

Foucault's concept of biopower builds on Goffman's analysis of the total institution. He describes the mechanisms of control in these settings as "an explosion of numerous and diverse techniques for achieving the subjugation of bodies and the control of populations" (Foucault 1978, 140). Foucault notes that institutions like schools, the police, and families help disseminate biopower that in turn guarantees "relations of domination and effects of hegemony" (1978, 141). He furthermore shows how these institutions build "mechanisms of observation . . . [that] penetrate into men's [people's] behavior" (1977, 204). Put simply, these institutions control inmates by training them to discipline and monitor themselves. As Goffman explains, institutions train individuals to accept a docile role while confined within them. Empirical research conducted in the United States suggests that Goffman's and Foucault's vision of the prison is consistent with what occurs in juvenile detention facilities (Bickel, 2010).[5]

Institutions also reproduce gender hierarchies, which complicate the experience of incarceration and detention for women and girls. Institutions of confinement in the United States have a unique history regarding girls and women. Historically, women and girls were incarcerated for participating in nonconforming gender behavior, like being unruly or expressing their sexuality (Pasko, 2010; Pasko, 2008; Mc-Daniels-Wilson and Belknap, 2008; Belknap, 2006; Bloom, Owen, and Covington, 2004; Bloom, Owen, Deschenes, and Rosenbaum, 2002; Gaarder and Belknap, 2002; Abrams, 2000). Established during the nineteenth century, these early detention facilities focused on training women, especially middle-class white women, to become better wives by adopting "appropriate" femininity (Davis, 2003).

The efforts of early women's jails were oriented toward "rehabilitating" women by training them to cook, clean, and sew (Davis, 2003).

In parallel with jails for adults, the juvenile justice system has a history of encouraging gender conformity and policing sexuality (Goodkind and Miller, 2006). In the early days of the juvenile justice system, most incarcerated girls were picked up for such offenses as "immorality" or "waywardness" (Abrams, 2000). Specifically, they might have been arrested for allegedly having participated in premarital sex or not submitting to the authority of their parents (Abrams and Curran, 2000). At these facilities, girls received gender-conforming training similar to that of women in prison; they were often incarcerated until they reached a "marriageable" age (Abrams, 2000). Girls today continue to be jailed for similar status offenses,[6] often at the request of their parents (Chesney-Lind and Shelden, 2004).

The history of women's incarceration becomes more complex when we consider how race, class, gender, and sexuality shape women's and girls' experiences with incarceration. Girls from working-class families and girls of color often suffer the brunt of punitive responses to violent behavior. Girls in detention centers are disproportionately poor and of color (Shelden, 2010). Consider, again, how women's prisons often aimed to "rehabilitate" middle-class white women and make them eligible for marriage. This same process trained poor women and women of color to become skilled domestic servants or to fulfill other racialized, classed, and gendered expectations (Goodkind, 2009). For white and middle-class women and girls, these institutions provided an opportunity to achieve a respectable femininity by learning domestic skills that would make them more marriageable. For these women, achieving a "respectable femininity" meant being submissive, tending to a home, and finding a husband. Conversely, these institutions have often expected girls of color to be "strong" and "mature" enough to take full responsibility for their "crimes" (Goodkind, 2009; Wacquant, 2002). While women were being taught similar skills, they were being prepared to achieve different goals shaped by their interlocking identities.

Considering these historical and political realities, it is not surprising that institutions of confinement continue to disproportionately punish girls of color. Even so, we lack a thorough understanding of the processes through which this takes place. Looking at the lives of Latina girls in their homes, schools, and detention centers allows us a glimpse of how race, class, gender, and incarceration influence the dynamics of violence and nonviolence in these facilities.

LIFE COURSE THEORY AND TURNING POINTS

In their classic study *Unraveling Juvenile Delinquency*, Sampson and Laub (1993) provide a "life course" analysis of deviance using data previously collected by Glueck and Glueck (1950). Scholars define the life course as "pathways through the age-differentiated life span," where age differentiation "is manifested in expectations and options that impinge on decision processes and the course of events that give shape to life stages, transitions, and turning points" (Elder, 1986, 17). "Turning points," or "hooks," are key moments when people transition away from deviant behavior (Giordano, Cernkovich, and Rudolph, 2002; Sampson and Laub, 1997; Sampson and Laub, 1993; Sampson and Laub, 1992).

In their classic 1993 study, Sampson and Laub applied the life course concept to a group of white "ethnic" men during the 1940s. Their life course theory was the first attempt to produce an explanation for participation in and desistance from crime during childhood, adolescence, and adulthood (Sampson and Laub, 1993; Sampson and Laub, 1992). They argue that delinquency at an early age produces weak social bonds with the adults in young people's lives. In turn, this lack of strong bonds contributes to young people's participation in further delinquency (Thornberry, 1997; Sampson and Laub, 1993; Sampson and Laub, 1992). Conversely, they argue that the increasing social bonds that come with getting married, starting a family, and finding a job make adults more likely to end their participation in crime and delinquency (Sampson and Laub, 1993). For young people, feeling strong bonds with family and school can contribute to desistance in crime *despite* structural factors such as previous incarceration, living in poverty, and attachment to deviant friends, or individual factors such as antisocial behavior or demonstrating aggressive childhood behavior (Thornberry, 1997; Sampson and Laub, 1993; Sampson and Laub, 1992).

Sampson and Laub's notion of social control is key to their discussion of turning points and criminal desistance. They define social control as "the capacity of a social group to regulate itself according to desired principles and values, enhanced to make norms and rules effective" (Sampson and Laub, 1993, 18). They use this concept to argue that pathways to crime are mediated by the social bonds individuals have with key institutions of social control like school, the family, and work (Sampson and Laub, 1997; Sampson and Laub, 1993; Sampson and Laub, 1992). Their understanding of these bonds is essential to my work, because it highlights the ways in which delinquent criminal behavior can have long-term, serious consequences for an individual's development and life course (Sampson and Laub, 1993; Thornberry, 1997).

More recently, researchers have attempted to build on "turning points" research to address criminal desistance in people of color, and especially young men of color (Fader, 2013). For example, Fader (2013), in her ethnography of young Black and Latino men in a reform school near Philadelphia, demonstrates how these individuals attempt to leave criminal pathways; some are successful and some are not. Fader shows how this trajectory is influenced by the multiple criminal justice institutions these young men negotiate. She also addresses the specific gendered challenges they face as they attempt to return to a traditional life course.

Sampson and Laub's (1993) theory, like most other works in studies of crime, focuses on men and boys (Fader, 2013; Thornberry, 1997; Sampson and Laub, 1992, Sampson and Laub, 1993). While many scholars of the life course approach have established clear patterns that often lead men and boys into delinquent behavior (Thornberry, 1997; Sampson and Laub, 1993; Sampson and Laub, 1992), their discussions of the involvement of women and girls in the criminal justice system often resemble an "add women and stir" approach (Chesney-Lind and Shelden, 2004; Chesney-Lind, 1986; Steffensmeir et al., 2005). A few researchers, however, have identified gendered pathways that lead into and away from crime (Giordano, Cernkovich, and Rudolph, 2002; Belknap, Holsinger, and Dunn 1997). By examining the experiences of young women, I interrogate the "turning points" component of life course theory discourse and complicate these ideas by also addressing issues of race, ethnicity, and gender.

In their groundbreaking 2002 study, Giordano, Cernkovich, and Rudolph identify some of the turning points for girls and women, using a mixed-method research approach with delinquent girls and women in Ohio. The authors use qualitative interview data to identify key environmental and cognitive shifts that help women and girls move away from a life of crime. They call these turning points "hooks for change," emphasizing the agency of the individual (Giordano, Cernkovich, and Rudolph, 2002, 1010). Their first key finding concerns readiness to change, especially in situations dealing with drug abuse (Giordano, Cernkovich, and Rudolph, 2002; Boyle, Polinsky, and Hser, 2000). Second is the requirement for a hook, or opportunity for change, whether a new job, a stable home, or some type of formal education. Third, individuals must begin to fashion a "replacement self" that can replace the prior, deviant self, which also entails a shift in attitude that allows girls and women to take advantage of an opportunity if it exists (Giordano, Cernkovich, and Rudolph, 2002). Fourth, individuals need to adopt a cognitive shift and no longer see deviant behavior as a positive or viable option (1002). In attempting to achieve this cognitive shift, women often adopt traditional replacement identities, like the "good wife" or "involved mother" or a "child of God." These new identities, however, can limit women's employment options and life choices (1053).

While these findings are important for this study of gender and criminal desistance, further research is still needed. For example, scholars still know little about how individuals' readiness to change is shaped or thwarted by police surveillance or wraparound services. Researchers also know too little about how girls and women leave criminal pathways when they have not experienced a cognitive shift that readies them for change. Finally, scholars are still building their understanding of how material and economic opportunities help or hinder young women's (and especially Latinas') ability to leave the criminal justice system. This book begins to explore these questions.

SURVEILLANCE IN SCHOOLS

Current research suggests that schools are adopting surveillance techniques that resemble those of lockdown facilities such as prisons. Schools are increasingly high-security environments with surveillance cameras, security guards, metal detectors, locker searches, drug-sniffing dogs, mandatory dress codes, and ID badges (Kim, Losen, and Hewitt, 2010; Bracy, 2010; Jones, 2010; Wald and Losen, 2003). In an ethnographic study based in

Minnesota, McGrew (2008) argues that more schools are turning into armed surveillance camps as the relationship between schools and detention centers grows. Until the recent past, this kind of surveillance was almost exclusively associated with poor urban schools (Winn, 2011). Although poor students and students of color continue to encounter the majority of this surveillance, this dynamic has begun to spread to middle- and upper-class, predominantly white schools as well (Bracy, 2010; Kupchik, 2009).

Cole and Heilig (2006) found that high-security school environments have become so normal that students have grown accustomed to hypersurveillance. Several scholars, including most notably Kupchik (2009), have argued that schools now prioritize finding and punishing school infractions over all other objectives. In his ethnographic research in four schools in the mid-Atlantic states, Kupchick found that current strategies for punishing misbehavior are "excessive and counterproductive" (2010, 4). Schools continue to adopt these practices despite evidence from scholars that strict surveillance exacerbates students' adverse behavior (Kupchik, 2010; Kupchik, 2009; Cole and Heilig, 2006).

The arrival of police inside of schools means that schools' disciplinary policies have stark and long-lasting effects on youth (Winn, 2011; Kim, Losen, and Hewitt, 2010; Bracy, 2010; Hirschfield, 2009; Price, 2009; McGrew, 2008; Wald and Losen, 2003; Casella, 2003). In a survey of literature on this topic, Hirschfield (2009) reports that many schools in urban areas have placed police departments in charge of school security. New York City, for example, has reached out to local law enforcement and established relationships with several police stations in the city and state (Casella, 2003). As a result, the school division of the NYPD is larger than Boston's entire police force (Hirschfield, 2009). These new school police are commonly referred to as school resource officers. Bracy's (2010) ethnographic study of two mid-Atlantic schools shows that these officers' duties include the traditional investigation of crimes, as well as less traditional roles such as mentoring students and teaching them to avoid drugs, alcohol, and violent encounters.

Most literature on this topic suggests that police on campus focus their time disproportionately on finding and punishing actual or perceived crimes (Winn, 2011; Bracy, 2010; Price, 2009; Hirschfield, 2009; McGrew, 2008). In

Winn's (2011) ethnographic study of girls in Atlanta, she states that once police are inside schools, they search and detain students for such minor infractions as carrying lighters. McGrew (2008) found that police officers now have access to students' school records and use this information to arrest them for trivial nonviolent behavior. As Bracy reports (2010), the presence of school resource officers on campus, and their partnership with school administrators, allows police officers to circumvent students' legal rights, particularly their right to refuse unlawful searches. The result is that, in American schools, police officers, instead of school officials, are increasingly dealing with perceived or actual "disruptive" behavior (Hirschfield, 2009; McGrew, 2008; Wald and Losen, 2003; Casella, 2003).

Alternative Education

Alternative schools, also known as "continuation schools," play a key role in the rise of surveillance in schools. Originally introduced as alternative high schools for students at risk of not graduating, continuation schools have flourished as a strategy for dealing with youth who have had exposure to the criminal justice system. Many students in continuation education are behind in high school credits or need flexible schedules because of work and family issues. These students are required to attend school at least three hours a day or a total of fifteen hours a week.

Continuation schools have become more popular nationwide (Kim, Losen and Hewitt, 2010; NAACP Legal Defense and Educational Fund 2005). According to a sociolegal study by Kim, Losen, and Hewitt (2010), somewhere between 600,000 and 1 million students in the United States currently attend alternative schools, at over 10,000 separate locations. In 2010, the state of California alone had 499 continuation schools (California Department of Education, 2012a), serving approximately 116,500 students during the academic year. A report published by Stanford University found that these schools service 10 percent of all students in the state and one out of every seven high school seniors (De Velasco and McLaughlin, 2012). A similar study found that 33 percent of all students who drop out of California high schools attend some form of alternative or continuation school (Rotermund, 2007).

Most school districts depict continuation schools as flexible alternatives for students with work or family problems (California Department of Education, 2012b). Once enrolled, however, students face new sets of challenges, including sexual harassment, random searches, drug testing, and potentially hostile peers (Simkins et al., 2004). Students enrolled in continuation schools, moreover, face increased surveillance and police contact that accelerates their path to incarceration (Farmer, 2010). These settings can also expose youth with existing behavioral problems to other students experiencing similar issues, further exacerbating the behaviors that schools initially intended to stop (De Velasco and McLaughlin, 2012; Winn 2011; McGrew 2008; NAACP Legal Defense and Educational Fund 2005). Students who have been placed in continuation schools seldom return to traditional high schools and are more likely to end up in community day schools (De Velasco and McLaughlin, 2012; Feierman, Levick, and Mody, 2009; Christle et al., 2005; Simkins et al., 2004).

Students' experiences in these schools are directly connected to their race, class, gender, sexuality, and academic ability. In California, Latino and Latina students make up a disproportionate number (56 percent) of students in continuation schools (Rios and Galicia, 2013; Malagon and Alvarez, 2010). Casella (2003) found that school districts place troubled youth, youth of color, and poor youth into special education programs and continuation schools. Bracy (2010) reports that boys, especially Black boys, are removed from traditional school environments and placed in continuation schools as a result of such small offenses as carrying a pocket knife. Cole and Heilig (2006) found that the bulk of students sent to continuation schools are children of color and children with disabilities. Cole and Heilig argue that removing struggling students from traditional schools "perpetuates a cycle of failure whereby students lose access to educational and social development opportunities and fall further behind" (2006, 321).

Latina youth in particular seem to be shuttled toward continuation schools. Bettie's (2003) study of Mexican American girls from towns in the great Central Valley of California, for example, found that pregnant girls and young mothers were encouraged to leave traditional schools and attend continuation schools. School staff took this approach in direct response to their perceptions of the girls as poor students with overactive sexuality and a lack of sexual morals (Bettie, 2003). In a qualitative study of Chicanas in continuation schools, Malagon and Alvarez (2010) found that school personnel paint working-class girls and girls of color in alternative education as hyper-sexualized; these personnel assume that only maladjusted and pregnant girls attend these educational institutions. Continuation schools often discourage students from attending by not paying attention to their needs or by telling students to stop attending school altogether (Simkins et al., 2004).

Community Day Schools

In California, community day schools are the newest version of continuation schools and alternative education. During the late 1990s, the State of California enacted legislation that required all expelled students to attend school, after a spike in expulsions produced a growing population of underage (under eighteen years of age) but unschooled young people. The same legislation authorized school districts to establish community day schools, like Legacy, to serve these expelled and other at-risk students. Designed to serve students who are labeled "troubled" or otherwise "unfit" by school, social service, or criminal justice officials, these schools have low student-teacher ratios. They are also expected to offer youth added support in the form of school counselors, psychologists, and academic and vocational training, as well as "pupil discipline" personnel. The students additionally receive support—or, less optimistically, supervision—from local education, law enforcement, probation, and human services agency personnel. Unlike traditional schools, these educational centers have been working directly with law enforcement agencies since their inception. Community day schools are the final option for students once they are expelled from their traditional high school or continuation school.

California provides a very specific set of requirements for the community day schools, to the point that the California Department of Education provides step-by-step instructions for how to start and fund such a school. From an administrative standpoint, the designation is desirable, because it captures additional state and local funding on top of regular school funding. Academically speaking, "students are expected to participate in academic programs that include high-level expectations from staff and students, and that are comparable to those available to students of similar age in the school district" (California Department of Education, 2013). Students at these schools are required to be in class at least 360 minutes every day and to participate in "academic programs that provide challenging curriculum and individual attention to student learning modalities and abilities." According to the state's website, community day schools are also supposed to promote social skills and self-esteem that will help students become productive adults.[7]

California clearly specifies where community day schools should be located. For example, the state website indicates that community day schools are separate schools, not merely separate programs within schools, and are intended to be located apart from other schools. Community day schools may not be situated on the same site as an elementary, middle, junior high, comprehensive senior high, opportunity, or continuation school (California Department of Education, 2013). While the state's promotional materials about the program highlight the added services students receive at community day schools, they downplay the requirement for legal segregation from traditional schools and their larger student bodies. As this book will make clear, youth at Legacy, and in the recuperation program specifically, are completely (and often permanently) isolated from traditional schools, students, and the opportunities they offer, with significant consequences for students' life courses.

Legacy is similar to other community day schools in that it works on a credit system. Students are given a set number of credits for every course they take. Since students at Legacy and El Valle don't often stay for an entire course, both institutions allow them to earn partial course credits. The students can earn credits through their traditional classes, independent study packets, or a credit recuperation computer program. This multitier approach to earning credits means some students can earn credits at an accelerated rate. This is important, since most youth in this program are generally short on credits.

To date, scholars have paid little attention to this new kind of school and its associated objectives. The published information I could find on the phenomenon was often in official reports written by educational agencies or nonprofit organizations. In fact, most of the information I gathered about community day schools came from analyzing school documents, from interviews and observations, and from the California Department of Education's website. Somewhat surprisingly, even researchers who examine the school-to-prison pipeline and surveillance in schools have overlooked these schools, usually lumping them together with other continuation schools if discussing them at all. Given the ubiquitousness and expanding presence of these schools in California and the rest of the United States, it is imperative to understand how these institutions affect students. This is especially the case for Latina and Latino students, who make up the majority of the student body in these sites in California. This book begins to inform scholars, policy analysts, and concerned citizens about the community day schools and their relationship to the continually changing landscape of American education.

KEY SETTINGS

This study is based on research conducted at two locations. I had initially planned to focus my research solely on El Valle Juvenile Detention Facility. After meeting me, however, an administrator at the jail invited me to also conduct fieldwork at Legacy Community Day School. A relationship similar to that between El Valle and Legacy can be found in sister institutions in almost every county in California (Flores, 2012). Given this, my findings provide researchers with key insights into the changing contours of public education and punishment throughout California, the most populous state in the nation.

El Valle Juvenile Detention Facility

Located forty miles outside of Los Angeles, California, El Valle was built on fifty acres of land in the last twenty years and can hold upward of four hundred youths. Youth are segregated by sex, and approximately 90 percent of the youth in this facility are boys. This means approximately forty girls are housed here daily. All the girls are held in one unit, completely segregated from the boys. The girls' unit is divided into "House One" and "House Two." House One holds juveniles whose cases have not been adjudicated or who will be in the facility for fewer than thirty days. House Two holds all other girls. Each cell in the facility can hold up to four people. The unit is connected to a recreational yard and a central communal space called a "day room," where the girls eat and interact with each other.

Approximately 95 percent of the girls at this facility are Latina; 4 percent are white; the other 1 percent of girls are Black or Asian. The girls at this facility range in age from eleven to nineteen. Most are from poor or working-class families with a history of incarceration and gang ties. This and other demographic information is displayed in table 1 in appendix 2. Girls here often have low academic skill levels and have not regularly attended school throughout their lives, a situation that is typical for incarcerated juveniles in the United States. For example, 34 percent of incarcerated U.S. youth were reported to have an educational disability, compared to 12.7 percent of students in public schools (Zabel and Nigro 2007). At El Valle, too, approximately a third of the girls reported an educational disability. All of the correctional staff who work in the girls' unit are women. While the facility does not allow men to supervise or teach in the girls' unit, they are allowed to substitute-teach or provide temporary assistance if a fight occurs.

Legacy Community School

Legacy is an example of a community day school. Although it has the capacity to serve 300 students, typically only about 150 students attend the school at any given time. It serves youth from sixth to twelfth grade, functioning as both a middle school and high school. In Legacy, 80 percent of students are Latino or Latina, and at least 66 percent of all students are classified by school officials as "socioeconomically disadvantaged." Students at Legacy have also struggled in the academic arena. For example, 92 percent of the students are below grade level in math or English. The school offers no advanced placement courses, and no student has ever met the requirements for any of the four-year California public universities. School officials have diagnosed approximately 15 percent of all students at Legacy with learning disabilities. The small school has a half-dozen classrooms and a small teaching staff. Given the student body's academic challenges, the resulting class sizes are smaller than in most schools and typically have ten to twenty-five students.

A large percentage of the student body at Legacy has had contact with the juvenile justice system at some point in their lives. This means that a substantial segment of this population is on formal probation or under other supervision or has at some point spent time in secure detention. At Legacy, unlike other, traditional schools, a steady flow of incoming and outgoing youth from the detention center in El Valle passes through the classrooms. It is school policy to put students in informal contact with a probation agent, even if they are not on formal probation. Boys and girls are drug-tested "every few weeks," according to the principal, but are also subject to random tests anytime they are on campus.

Like other community day and continuation schools, Legacy struggles with high student suspension rates. The year before I began fieldwork, Legacy recorded twelve hundred suspensions in one year, a staggering number for any school, but especially shocking for one with an average of only 150 students present. In order to curtail this trend, the school started a new in-school suspension program. School officials sent students to this program for "small" offenses like tardiness or dress-code violations. According to one school official, these changes have reduced the number of out-of-school suspensions to nine hundred in one year.

Legacy Community Day School and El Valle Juvenile Detention Facility are inextricably connected. These institutions are so closely linked that administrators refer to El Valle as Legacy's sister institution. For example, Plazo, the gender-segregated correctional school that exists within El Valle, shares a principal with Legacy. The administrator splits his time between the two institutions. As is common throughout California, the community day school and the correctional school use a synchronized curriculum. In other words, youth who are incarcerated are doing the same work, using the same materials, and moving at the same pace as individuals who attend Legacy.

Students who spend more than fifteen days at El Valle detention center have to attend Legacy once they are released, "because the regular school won't take them," says one of the instructors in El Valle. In other words, not only were youth in my study punished at El Valle, but they were also doubly punished by having to attend Legacy, which some teachers feel is "a dumping ground for all of the schools that don't want their kids." Given the close links between the two institutions, Legacy began moving toward a "self-contained model" for "transition and reentry." In other words, Legacy started to focus its attention almost exclusively on students who had been incarcerated. While doing so has certain benefits for students, it also increases the chances that young people will likely enter Legacy, and not their traditional or even a continuation school, once released from incarceration. This process has already started with the establishment of the Recuperation Class.

Recuperation Class

This self-contained program within Legacy is for youth with "drug dependence and other behavioral issues." All the youth in this class are on formal probation, and most have been incarcerated. The "self-contained" aspect of this class means that students in this room do not speak with, take breaks with, or otherwise mingle with the other youth at Legacy. Furthermore, these students receive instruction in every subject in the same classroom, and always by the same teacher, Janet Powell. The local probation department directly funds this ten-person class, in contrast to the rest of the school, which is funded by the county and the state. In this unique setting, the teacher provides instruction as the probation agent walks around, randomly pulling out students to conduct drug tests, to question them about their behavior outside of school, or to take them directly to El Valle. This probation officer is permanently stationed inside the class.

For all intents and purposes, the Recuperation Class operates as its own semi-independent entity. The Legacy School makes separate rules for the class's students and can also change their academic schedules. For example, the larger Legacy School shuts down for the summer. The Recuperation Class, however, stays open and attendance is mandatory. This summer session is completely funded by the probation department. The funding pays for a separate teacher to provide instruction, as well as money for student meals and any other additional costs. Interestingly, circumstance suggests that this local probation department had the economic resources to change the traditional school year. Requiring that students in this class attend school throughout the summer resulted in their uninterrupted policing.

The Recuperation Class is the key location in which the concept of what I am calling wraparound incarceration plays out. The Los Angeles County Department of Children and Family Services defines wraparound services as "an integrated, multi-agency, community-based philosophy of unconditional commitment to support families to safely and competently care for their children. The single most important outcome of the wraparound approach is a child thriving in a permanent home and supported by normal community services and informal supports" (2009, 1). The El Valle Probation Department has adopted a similar approach in working with young people. There, the multiagency wraparound services include the detention center, placement homes, electronic monitoring, and the Legacy School itself—especially the Recuperation Class.

METHODS

Over the course of twenty-four months, I conducted ethnographic research at these two sites. I used four strategies for collecting data at both field sites. I began this investigation with fieldwork at El Valle Juvenile Detention Facility (2009–2011) and later at Legacy Community Day School (2010–2011). I engaged in participant observation for approximately two years and gathered five hundred pages of single-spaced notes before conducting interviews or collecting additional data. This allowed me to restructure my previous research design to address the issues that most commonly appeared at both sites, particularly the violence that exists at every stage of young women's lives and their negative experiences in the educational setting. Once I reached this saturation point using field notes, I began conducting focus groups at both sites.

I conducted approximately eight focus groups in detention and three at the community day school. These groups had between four and ten participants and allowed me to test some of my future interview questions. Engaging with the groups also allowed me to develop several working theories and preliminary hypotheses. It was during these group interviews that I discovered the connections between my two field sites. This unexpected finding helped me broaden the scope of my study in a way that allowed me to unravel the increasing connection between juvenile detention and community day schools, a phenomenon that remains understudied by scholars.

After collecting this preliminary data, I conducted forty-four in-depth semistructured interviews with thirty different incarcerated girls. Each formal interview and focus group lasted between one and three hours, with most lasting about an hour and a half. At El Valle, I conducted these interviews inside a soundproof interview room that teachers, counselors, and probation officers use in order to meet with detainees. For my interviews at Legacy, I chose a quiet communal space or an empty classroom. The girls provided consent for these interviews, and I notified their parents by mail about my work. After sending the notification, I waited for two weeks before conducting an interview, to give parents the opportunity to decline or consent to it. These interviews allowed me to identify girls' initial contact with the criminal justice system. They also shed light on the processes that lead girls in and out of the criminal justice system. These one-on-one interviews allowed young women to share information they did not feel comfortable addressing during group interviews.

I also formally interviewed three teachers, several administrators, counselors, probation officers, and teaching assistants, and attempted to interview correctional officers.[8] These interviews with formal actors in both of the facilities allowed me to better understand the challenges these individuals face. They also allowed me to develop an understanding of the formal goals of the detention center and the community day school. Institutional actors in this setting often had altruistic goals for the young women in their charge; however, for the young women in my study, these goals often resulted in punitive outcomes.

I transcribed field notes, focus groups, and interviews verbatim. I then used Dedoose, a qualitative software package, to code these documents, with special attention to how youth in these settings discussed their experiences in home, school, detention, and in the community day school. My analysis also included a through examination of "negative cases," or alternative explanations. When I was confronted with a negative case, I addressed it in the text or incorporated it into my larger analysis. Looking for alternative explanations in my study ultimately strengthened my findings and my larger project. This method of analyzing ethnographic data follows the process described in Emerson, Fretz, and Shaw (1995).

The young people I spoke with all discussed similar themes, with very little variation. I also collected historical and secondary data by analyzing official documents with information on each girl's age, educational level, disabilities (if any), race or ethnicity, and the amount of time she had been incarcerated. These documents allowed me to verify the information I gathered during interviews. Furthermore, the answers I received during interviews and focus groups were consistent with the information I gathered in field notes, in secondary documents, and through informal interviews with teachers and correctional guards. This "triangulation," or multiple-method approach, allowed me to combat the instances where "people's behavior doesn't always match their words" (Esterberg, 2002, 36). A more detailed discussion of methodological issues can be found in the appendix.

CHAPTER OVERVIEW

In the first chapter, I illustrate how girls' experiences at home led to their eventual incarceration. Most girls in this study experienced physical, sexual, or psychological abuse at the hands of their parents or guardians. These experiences pushed girls into unhealthy, intimate partner relationships. When these new unions failed, girls often turned to drugs to cope with their tumultuous home life and the loss of their new partners. While these findings are not entirely new, I trace how girls' home experiences spilled over into intimate-partner violence and their eventual incarceration. These specific home experiences fundamentally altered girls' life trajectories before and after they entered the educational and criminal justice systems.

The second chapter considers what takes place once girls are arrested and brought to El Valle Detention Center. While studies identify some of the key pathways that lead young people to incarceration, few of these works describe how young people's lives change once they are incarcerated. I discuss how correctional staff and other staff members in El Valle encourage, condone, and co-opt violence to achieve their own institutional and personal goals, which are typically oriented toward efforts to control girls' behavior and, according to staff, to maintain the safety and order of the institution. I also demonstrate the multiple strategies girls use to navigate interpersonal and institutional forms of violence.

As noted above, girls who spend more than fifteen days at El Valle almost uniformly end up at Legacy Community Day School. Chapter 3 describes the girls' experiences at this nominally education-oriented facility. Here, girls are searched, made to walk through metal detectors, placed on formal or informal probation, and subjected to perpetual contact from criminal justice agents. Legacy School officials have granted the local probation office unfettered access to their students in return for financial support. The chapter describes how the process of wraparound incarceration plays out through the formal surveillance procedures of the Legacy School, particularly in its Recuperation Class. Young women move back and forth between this school and secure detention.

In chapter 4, I describe how girls' contact with the criminal justice system continues, even for those lucky few who transition back to traditional school. Having spent extended periods of time at Legacy and El Valle, the young women in my study struggled in a more traditional environment. For example, girls who experience abuse or who have previously been incarcerated often act out by overtly expressing their sexuality, fighting with other students, arguing with teachers, or experimenting with drugs. Once school officials notice this "unladylike," or nonconforming, gender behavior, girls are labeled as "at risk" or "problem" students. These institutional labels led the young women in my study to be targeted for exclusionary discipline, which inevitably resulted in their return to Legacy Community School. School administrators and police collectively suspend and expel students from school, but they never address the trauma or challenges of being institutionalized.

Some girls do manage to escape from this system of wraparound incarceration. In chapter 5, I identify the key turning points that allowed a few girls in my study to transition from detention to college or gainful employment or, less happily, the larger California prison system. I also reveal the key moments in girls' development when they are ready for and willing to undertake positive change. Many youth are, unfortunately, so entrenched in the criminal justice system that exiting that system becomes impossible, even when they are ready for change. This final section also sheds light on the key factors that educators and criminal justice agencies can look for when attempting to make positive interventions in young people's life trajectories.

The concluding chapter focuses on the theoretical and empirical findings of this study, including the implications of the concept of wraparound incarceration for future research.

CHAPTER 1

Trouble in the Home, and First Contact with the Criminal Justice System

Ray is a nineteen-year-old, fourth-generation[1] Latina. She was born in a community adjacent to El Valle Juvenile Detention Facility. She, like many of the girls in my study, was part of a family struggling with intergenerational poverty, unemployment, and poor housing conditions in a segregated neighborhood. I first met Ray early in my research. She is about five foot seven and extremely thin. When I met her, she had dark wavy hair, but she eventually shaved her head. This new look served as a marker of sexuality and neighborhood affiliation. I would joke and tell her, "I had the same haircut when I was your age!" She jokingly replied, "Damn! Why are you talking smack?"

During our first meeting inside of El Valle, she said nothing. She walked sluggishly around class, could barely stand to sharpen her pencil, and looked as if she weighed around one hundred pounds. As a researcher new to this detention center, I wondered what was wrong with her. Ms. Sanchez, the classroom teacher, sat next to me and explained, "She just got here yesterday. She ran away and is detoxing now. She has a big meth problem."

During our first interview, I asked Ray to tell me her life story. Her response speaks to an overwhelming theme among justice-involved young women. For young girls, trouble in the criminal justice systems typically begins at home: "My life story . . . I don't know how to describe it. . . . Well, I grew up poor, big family, single mom always depending on partners; started getting in trouble at school 'cause we never stayed long." When Ray was young, her mother struggled to take care of her children. She had to constantly move to escape abusive partners or to find more affordable housing for her family and herself. Given this constant shifting, Ray did not attend school regularly. On top of this instability she, like the other young women in my study, experienced multiple forms of abuse that hastened her contact with the criminal justice system. As I got to know Ray, she told me about her path from home, to school, to detention, to community day school, and eventually, to the larger California corrections system.

Ray's path is depressingly typical. In this chapter, I draw on feminist criminology and research on gender and crime to demonstrate how abuse and neglect in the home led the young women in my study to their first contact with the criminal justice system. I pay attention to how home instability is shaped by gendered, racialized, and class-specific challenges.

This chapter as a whole begins to show the shortcomings of wraparound services. Although these services are intended to help girls at home and school, they did not provide support to the girls in my study. Once girls became involved with the criminal justice system, these services often provided punishment instead of support.

TROUBLE IN THE HOME

A large portion of the girls I interviewed experienced sexual abuse in the home, or in their community, or both. For the young women who experienced abuse in the home, their abusers were usually parents or other family members, as is so often the case with sexual abuse. For young women associated with the criminal justice system, sexual abuse is almost always perpetrated by a relative or close acquaintance (Winn, 2011; Winn, 2010; Chesney-Lind and Shelden, 2014; Simkins et al., 2004; Kakar, Friedemann, Peck, 2002). Scholars have also found that Latina girls are more likely to be sexually abused than Black or white girls (González-López, 2006). Rates of prior sexual abuse are extremely high among incarcerated Latinas (Díaz-Cotto, 2006), including the girls in my study.

Ray, like many of the girls in my study, experienced sexual abuse at the hands of multiple family members and neighbors. The first time she mentioned these experiences, she said, "I think it all started when I was seven, . . . when I started being really bad. . . . I went to go live with my dad for a little bit, 'cause we were homeless. . . . I had to go stay with him, and he had just got out of prison; and then something happened. . . . He molested me, . . . and then I went to go live back with my mom." Her mother, who was homeless at the time, believed it would be better for Ray to stay in her father's apartment than to live on the streets. When Ray told her mother that her father was sexually abusing her, her mother removed her from her father's house. Together, they wandered to various friends' and family members' homes.

Ray continued to experience sexual abuse by multiple family members and neighbors as her mother attempted to find stable housing. According to her, these events directly influenced her behavior. She began to "act up" during the times where she experienced sexual abuse.

The youth in my study also experienced psychological abuse in their homes. Debby is a sixteen-year-old Latina with a copper complexion. The tattoos on her face and arms give her a menacing look, hiding what I know is a warm personality. Debby, unlike the other girls at the facility, was a deeply entrenched gang member of a local Mexican transnational gang. During our interview, she eagerly recounted her life story, which focused largely on the psychological abuse she experienced at the hands of her father. As an eight-year-old, Debby recalled, she had one of the most frightening experiences of her short life. She explained that her father was diagnosed with both cancer and schizophrenia, and that he would regularly become psychologically abusive to his children and physically abusive to Debby's mother.

One evening after arriving home, her father went directly into her mother's room. Her siblings heard her mother yell. Debby said, "I was so scared. I didn't wanna go up to my dad's room, 'cause my dad was really scary." Debby and her siblings went to investigate, and Debby recalled, "My dad, I guess he forgot to lock the door; and *entramos* [we entered], and we just saw my dad with a belt in his hand, and my mom's face is all bruised up. We were all: '*Papi* [Daddy], stop, stop, stop'; and my dad was all: 'What are you doing out of bed? Get your asses back in bed. Fuck you guys.' Like he wasn't fully there. And I got scared; it was the first time he was talking to me like that." Debby recounts how she and her siblings saw their mother beaten and bruised. Apparently her father had beaten her with a leather belt because he felt she was being unfaithful.

Debby's grandfather, who lived next door, managed to intervene in this fight, and things calmed down.

The next morning, however, resulted in more traumatic events. Her father decided that he had had his fill of his family and packed his things. He loaded his truck and grabbed Debby's youngest brother and sped off. He had decided to return to Mexico and had kidnapped her brother in the process. During the trip, the child's crying angered her father, so he pushed him out of the car while driving on the freeway. Luckily, her brother survived, but after this event Debby did not see her father again. She told me that, upon her father's departure, she began to struggle with delusions and depressions similar to the psychotic events her father experienced. As had been the case for Ray, the psychological abuse in Debby's family began to influence her home life.

Virginia, like Ray and Debby, experienced abuse in a very turbulent home. However, her abuse was mostly physical and gender-specific. For example, as the eldest daughter in the home, she was expected to cook, clean, and care for her younger siblings. If she did not complete these gender-specific tasks or challenged her parents, she was beaten. Virginia was placed in charge of tending her young siblings from a very early age because of her parents' alcoholism and drug abuse.

Virginia is about five foot five, a sixteen-year-old first-generation U.S. Latina with a fallow complexion and timid personality. When I asked her to share her life story, she described a lifetime of abuse and mistreatment. When Virginia was eight years old, her family moved to El Valle, California, from central Mexico. Shortly after this move, she recalled, "my parents, they drank more; my mom became an alcoholic. And then they would hit me, and Dad and Mom would fight. When I was . . . twelve to fifteen, the violence got worse. . . . My mom became a meth addict and an alcoholic. That ruined our life." The violence Virginia experienced became progressively worse with every passing year. Slowly her parents' addictions got so bad that they stopped feeding her and her siblings altogether. As the oldest daughter, Virginia did her best to feed her young brother and sister. She did this by panhandling, selling her mother's alcohol outside of a local liquor store, and asking neighbors for help. This situation began putting a strain on the lives of her growing siblings as well.

During this time, Virginia herself became increasingly frustrated and violent. She recalled that she started "boxing" her dad and fighting back against abuse. In a separate incident, she attempted to protect her younger sister, who was in turn trying to defend herself from their mother: "She was pretty violent. She would hit me with anything she could get her hands on . . . plates, cups. . . . And then she shattered my sister's bone with a broom. . . . She whacked her with it, and she shattered her bone." While Virginia was accustomed to her parents' physical assaults, she was extremely upset that her mother broke her younger sister's wrist. Clearly, the violence was getting worse.

Approximately a year after this incident, an anonymous source notified child protective services. Virginia and her siblings were removed from their home and placed in a group home supervised by social workers. Once law enforcement officials became aware of the abuse, they arrested her mother, who was subsequently deported. Virginia remained in the group home for more than a year, after which she and her siblings returned to live with her father, who continued to mistreat them.

ROMANTIC PARTNERS AND TROUBLE IN THE HOME

The young women in my study often sought out a romantic partner to help them deal with the emotional and physical abuse they experienced in their parents' homes. These new partnerships were often short-lived, and they frequently created multiple problems for the girls, both inside and outside their homes. Eventually these new relationships pulled girls away from their home lives and pushed them into high-risk behavior. For the girls in my study, a new romance represented the possibility for a "normal" life away from the abuse they'd experienced. It also allowed them to gain the emotional support they did not receive from their families. In the end, however, these new relationships seldom worked out.

Feliz is a seventeen-year-old, third-generation, light-skinned Latina. She has brown hair that hangs down to her waist and a friendly and outgoing personality. She is five foot six with a slender build. She began experiencing trouble the summer she transitioned from middle school to high school. Her home life was complicated by the problems that existed between her abusive father and her mother, who used drugs. Feliz's mother and father fought a lot, not so much because of her mother's drug use, but because of her father's infidelity and work in the informal economy. She said, "I guess he [her father] would cheat on my mom a lot; and to keep my mom settled and content and pretty much oblivious, . . . he'd bring her bags of bud [marijuana] . . . and she'd smoke." Feliz's father attempted to control her mother by offering her large amounts of sedatives and opiates, which he also sold. He also verbally abused her mother and her other siblings. Eventually, her family was evicted from their apartment in Los Angeles, and they moved to El Valle. After this, Feliz's father commuted forty miles to the Los Angeles city core to continue his dual employment. Her mother became a homemaker for the family, and they attempted to start a new life away from her father's drug dealing and indiscretions.

For a brief period, Feliz's home situation improved, largely because of the absence of her father. Things were "getting better" all around for her and her family. Her mother, however, continued to use drugs. Although Feliz was at first too young to remember her mother's drug use, she identified this behavior once she became an adolescent: "I noticed that my mom would sneak around the house a lot and into the backyard and stuff. Now I look back and I know she'd always be smoking bud." The challenges Feliz experienced at home became worse when she began a new relationship with Edwin, a boy who attended her middle school. She said, "I got a boyfriend who I fell in love with."

Feliz and this boy dated for approximately a year. During this time she started sneaking out of her home to visit her boyfriend. One evening, Feliz left to visit Edwin. Upon her return home, she found both of her parents waiting for her—they had discovered her late-night exit. "I got caught, and my dad was beating me because I was sneaking out to go see Edwin. . . . He beat me pretty bad." Feliz's unannounced exit, her new relationship, and her father's perception of what he took to be her inappropriate sexual behavior resulted in a severe beating that left Feliz emotionally and physically exhausted. Her perception of her father changed as she recalled that she had had "bruises everywhere." Feliz's experience is consistent with most of the literature on girls' physical, psychological, and sexual abuse in the home, which suggests that abuse often begins or intensifies after girls express their sexuality and begin new intimate relationships (Winn, 2011; Winn, 2010; Sharma, 2010; Chesney-Lind and Shelden, 2014).

If her father had hoped to convince Feliz to stop seeing Edwin, his plan backfired. She lost respect for her father and became more attached to Edwin. Unfortunately, her father's abusive behavior continued and reached a tipping point shortly after her initial beating. A few days after this incident, Feliz planned to go see a movie, but her father refused to let her leave. Feliz and her father began to argue, and she said, "Can you not be an asshole?!" This infuriated her dad; "he started hitting me, and it didn't stop till I got to my room, which is down the hallway and up the stairs." A concerned neighbor called the police, who arrived at the home shortly afterward. When law enforcement officials entered Feliz's home, they noticed her visible signs of abuse. They arrested her father and began to question the family. Feliz recalled, "I had bruises everywhere, so the only reason my mom didn't get arrested is because she was like, 'I can't leave her, look at her. Look at her body, she has bruises, she has cuts. . . . Her dad beats her.'" Since Feliz's mother was her only other guardian, the police decided not to arrest her and blamed Feliz's father entirely for his daughter's bad physical state.

Feliz's father was taken to county jail, and Feliz herself was taken to the police station. At the station she was questioned, and "they took pictures of me and my body. . . . He [her father] got charged with child battery or child endangerment." At fourteen, then, Feliz had her first encounter with the criminal justice system. At the station she was photographed and the police documented her physical condition. This information was then used to prosecute her father. She remembered this as "one of the worst days of her life."

The pattern that I describe here was the overarching narrative for the youth in my study. Girls experience abuse in the home and look for ways to spend less time there. Then, the girls begin expressing their sexuality by meeting a partner at school or in the community, and they begin sneaking out of their homes or staying out late. Their new partners provide them with an escape and the emotional support they do not receive from their families. This in turn results in more abuse at the hands of already violent parents, who disapprove of these new relationships. At this point the young women begin to act out further—mostly by continuing to date despite their parent's disapproval and physical punishment.

Debby, introduced above, similarly began dating at a very early age. She was eleven and Daniel was seventeen years old. Debby kept this new relationship from her mother, knowing she would disapprove. In the beginning, she was content with her relationship with Daniel. She said, "[At first] he would come to see me; he would buy me ice cream. He would take me everywhere with him. He was like, 'Oh baby, I love you. You mean the world to me.' *No sabía nada* [I didn't know anything]." However, this changed one evening when her boyfriend called her on the phone: "It's fucking one o'clock in the morning. . . . I met with him near the graveyard. He just told me: . . . 'I have a surprise, but you have to promise me that you will do it.' He's like, 'Pinky swear, pinky promise, cross your heart, hope to die.' And we ended up doing it [sleeping together]. It was the most horrible experience ever. I hated it, I was crying. It was horrible. I just didn't like it. And two weeks later, . . . I ended up going again."

Early in her relationship with Danny, Debby enjoyed the attention and the escape from the emotional trauma she previously experienced. This changed the evening she first had intercourse. She felt coerced into this "horrible" act. Although she agreed initially, she soon refused his multiple requests. After she turned him down, he stopped contacting her. She said, "He 'hit it and quit it' [slept with me and left], so I'm like, 'Okay.' *Nunca* [never], it never processed that he would do that shit to me. . . . And I guess he didn't use a condom on the first time or the second time, I don't know. Three weeks [later] . . . I found out I was pregnant."

Now eleven-year-old Debby had to confront her mother with the news. Her mother became angry and hysterical. Debby recalled that her mother asked, "'Who's your boyfriend ? Who's your boyfriend?' And I'm like, 'Daniel.'" . . . [But he was] all tatted up. So she knew he was older than seventeen. It was my *primera vez* [first time], and I'm all, 'He loves me. He loves me.' *Pero* [But] fuck no, that fool left me." Debby's mother was infuriated, on multiple counts. First, she knew Debby's "boyfriend." Daniel was an adult, and Debby was only a girl. She also knew this man would not or could not care for the child he and her daughter conceived. She was, moreover, furious that Debby would have a boyfriend and experience sex at such a young age. Finally, Debby's mother had neither the material resources to take care of another child nor the space in her crowded house for another person.

This last point is critical to understanding what went wrong in the girls' lives. A supportive parent, living in a healthy home environment, would likely have been in a better position to deal with Debby's new pregnancy. For instance, she might have had Daniel arrested for statutory rape, or she might have counseled her daughter in the various options (adoption, terminating the pregnancy) that were available to her. Her mother also could have offered to listen to Debby or to take her to see a therapist. But this did not describe Debby's mother, who, moreover, lacked financial resources, social networks, and education. She found herself navigating the same kinds of situations that Duck (2012) describes for poor, Black, inner-city women. These women must negotiate a constant set of economic, policy, and family instabilities while using informal support. In the end, Debby's mother sent the baby to live with members of their extended family.

In the meantime, Debby experienced multiple forms of abuse at the hands of her family members, both during and after her pregnancy. This abuse started when her mom pressured her to have an abortion. Debby refused and insisted on keeping her child. After she refused to get an abortion, her brother told her, "'If you don't have an abortion, I will make you get an abortion.' . . . He beat me up so many times, *pero* [but] he [the baby] still came out. It was just amazing, holding something that came out of you. . . . He is yours, and no one is going to take him away." She miraculously carried her child to full term, despite the regular beatings she received from her mother and brother in an attempt to make her miscarry. Within a month after the baby was born, her mother insisted that she "get that kid out of the house." Eventually her mother gave her two options: give her child to members of their extended family in Mexico, or be kicked out of the house entirely. Shocked by these recent events, Debby attempted to contact Daniel, only to find out that he was incarcerated in a Mexican jail. Not knowing what else to do, she eventually allowed her mother to take her child to family members in Mexico. Initially, Debby's family went south and visited the small child regularly. Over time, however, these trips became less and less frequent, and eventually the child did not recognize Debby as his actual mother. This had a devastating effect on Debby, who felt she had lost her child completely.

Debby's case also illustrates some of the gender-specific forms of interpersonal violence girls experience in the home. While Debby's case might seem like an extreme example, early pregnancy was a common occurrence for the youth in my study. Ray, for example, also had a baby. As a twelve-year-old, she was completely unprepared to be a mother. As had happened in Debby's case, the child's father was a justice-involved older man who was incarcerated for an extended period after she gave birth. Ray's situation was exacerbated by her mother's lack of resources and an unstable housing situation. After Ray had her child, her mom pressured her to find employment to provide for her new baby; they began to fight regularly. Ray then began running away from home, and her mother eventually took custody of Ray's son, often refusing to let her visit her child. For young women like Ray and Debby, getting pregnant further complicated their already challenging lives at home. Their lack of economic resources meant that they had to stay home and deal with this mistreatment if they wanted to stay in contact with their children.

Girls who violated heteronormative expectations also found themselves in trouble at home. Bonita, for example, initially started getting in trouble in the eighth grade. She is a third generation Latina. At five foot five and about 120 pounds, she looks innocuous and quiet from a distance. When she opens her mouth to speak, however, you know better: she has a loud, booming voice and an energetic personality. When I asked her about her experience, she responded, "I started dating, . . . and my mom did not approve, 'cause I was with a girl. And my mom, she doesn't go to church or nothing, she is not religious—she just didn't condone it." Bonita identifies this moment as key in her life's trajectory. In this case, her mother did not disapprove of her daughter dating; she merely disapproved of her dating another young woman. This event created tension between Bonita and her mother, since Bonita continued dating her girlfriend. Ironically, her mother runs a group home for girls, but this did not help Bonita. Instead, her mother used her insider knowledge of the placement and criminal justice system to punish Bonita by having her locked up. For example, she kicked Bonita out of the house and then told law enforcement officials that her daughter had run away. Her mother continued to punish Bonita for her behavior and, ultimately, kicked her out of her home permanently.

Situations like these are tremendously important. Dating other young women and getting pregnant at eleven years of age violate ideas of respectable feminine behavior for Latinas. Latino cultural ideals dictate that young women should remain virgins until they are married, and that they should be submissive and show deference to authority figures (Garcia, 2012; Dietrich, 1998; Segura, 1993; Soto, 1986; Fox, 1983). Garcia (2012) poignantly addresses how these ideals of Latina femininity are outdated and erroneous, but young girls continue to be held to these standards. The experiences of Feliz, Debby, Ray, and Bonita demonstrate how young Latina women are punished by their parents for violating gendered expectations.

Sooner or later, these experiences begin to negatively influence girls' behavior. Often, they hasten girls' contact with the criminal justice system. For most of the girls in my study, their romantic contacts, and the resulting tension with their families, pushed them toward the beginning of serious substance abuse.

BEGINNING SUBSTANCE ABUSE

Drug addiction was ubiquitous among my research subjects. Most of the girls in my study began using a cocktail of psychotropic drugs, barbiturates, and sedatives at a very early age. They also experienced moderate-to-severe methamphetamine dependence. Commonly known as "meth," this highly addictive drug led many of the girls in my study to their first arrest. And because the girls in my study experienced unstable home lives, they were more likely to use on the streets, where they were more apt to be arrested for their drug use.

While high rates of girls' and boys' arrests for drug use are well established in the academic literature (Chesney-Lind and Shelden, 2014), scholars know less about how the drug addiction begins. This is especially the case for Latino and Latina adolescents. Most of the young women in my study began using drugs around the time they transitioned from elementary to middle school, between the ages of nine and fifteen. Most of these girls began using drugs to deal with trauma at home, or because a family member introduced them to drugs, or to deal with the loss of a romantic partner.

Maria is a fifteen-year-old, third-generation Latina. She has a sepia complexion and hair dyed green, pink, and purple, and she stands about five and a half feet tall. I first met her a year into my research in El Valle. She sported several punk-band tattoos on her hands and forearms, and these tattoos were surrounded by scars from frequent self-mutilation. Despite these unnerving marks on her body, she appeared to be happy and greeted me with enthusiastic questions about my favorite bands. During our interview, she discussed the beginning of her drug use and the abuse she experienced in her home.

Maria first began having problems when her mother started dating. Maria and her mother's boyfriend did not get along and began fighting. Then Maria started fighting with her older sister, who tried to choke her during an altercation. Fed up with this behavior, Maria's mother sent her away to live with her grandmother. Maria told me, "I got kicked out of my house when I was fourteen, and [I] started drinking a lot. And I think I started doing Triple C's and started popping pills. . . . I was just partying all day with my friends, and . . . I started drinking a lot, like everyday . . . as soon as I woke up until I passed out, . . . taking whatever pills, whatever fucked me up." "Triple C" refers to Coricidin HBP, a cough and cold medicine. When taken in excess, this drug produces powerful hallucinations and numbing dissociation (U.S. Department of Justice, 2003). Maria combined this with other sedatives and pharmaceutical-grade pills, which, along with the lack of supervision once she left her grandmother's house, started her on a path to serious drug use and subsequent addiction. Without the ability to return to her home, Maria continued this behavior for an extended period, eventually squatting in an abandoned building with her friend.

Aracely is a slender seventeen-year-old, third-generation Latina. She comes from a family with intergenerational ties to a local gang. During our interview she described the beginning of the drug use that ultimately landed her in the detention center. Aracely, like Feliz, Ray, Debby, and Virginia, began her drug use to deal with the abuse she experienced at home. She first began experiencing problems when her father sent her to live with family in Texas. Aracely, who is the product of an extramarital affair, felt that she was often treated "worse" by her father and other family members and physically abused for trivial reasons. Periodically in her life, she had moved back and forth between Texas and California; and during one of her extended stays in California, she noticed that her sister and other extended family members would lock themselves in a small room for hours at a time. She soon learned that they used meth in this room and were attempting to keep this fact from her.

I asked her, "How old were you when you started using meth?" She replied,

> When I was twelve. . . . I didn't have to walk anywhere to use drugs. I could just ask a family member. I remember knocking on the door, and at first they wouldn't let me in, and then finally they let me in. . . . I asked what they were doing, and . . . they pulled out shit [meth], you know? They were crushing it, and then they asked me if I wanted one. . . . I remember first snorting it, and I just remember that, after that, I was doing it with my friend until they [Aracely's parents] caught me. . . . That's when I started using drugs all crazy.

Aracely's experiences provide us with an inside look into the beginning stages of drug abuse. Initially, she was curious about her siblings' secretive activities. Eventually her half brothers and half sisters invited her to use meth for the first time as a twelve-year-old elementary-school student. Her drug use continued uninterrupted until her father caught her and her sister smoking together in their backyard. Infuriated by her behavior, her father beat her and then sent her to Texas, where she started using drugs "all crazy." This drug binge had several negative effects for her home and academic life, as well as on her health. The lack of parental supervision, easy access to drugs, and the fact that family members used meth facilitated the drug addiction that she has struggled with for the past seven years.

Drug use increased drastically among the girls in my study once they began dating. While some studies suggest that boyfriends or male partners often introduce girls to drug use (Carbone-Lopez and Miller, 2012; Lopez, Jurik, and Gilliard-Matthews, 2009; Díaz-Cotto, 2006; Benda, 2005), this was not the case for my research subjects. Most of the young women first experimented with drugs with their family members. It is true, however, that their drug use often increased exponentially when they began spending time with a romantic partner. This was the case for Sandra, a fifteen-year-old, first-generation Latina with a very light complexion. I first met her in a focus group, where she discussed having been shot in the neck with a gun. Like the other girls in my study, she began using drugs and alcohol at home. Her father first got her drunk when she was nine years old. By twelve she was abusing prescription pills, and by fourteen she was using methamphetamine regularly. Her drug habit became worse when she started dating a local drug dealer. Her new boyfriend became controlling and abusive and would refuse to let her leave the house for days on end. She told me,

> He would just occupy me in here [his house]. [He would say,] "Babe, here's a sack, smoke yourself away." . . . [It was] horrible, horrible [pause]. He would take me hostage. . . . [I would say,] "Well, I want to go to my mom's friend's house only for a while." [But] he's all smoked out, all heroined out, . . . and he's like, "You can't leave! You can't leave!" And I was like, "Okay, yes I can." He's like, "No! No you can't!" And then he's like, "If you leave just watch what happens!" . . . I wouldn't see the sun for five days.

Sandra describes how her life changed with her new boyfriend. Initially, her new partner was fun and caring. However, he quickly became paranoid and feared someone would target Sandra because of his drug business. His excessive meth and heroin use also made him manic and violent. To keep her busy during the periods when he insisted that she not leave his home, he would supply her with a steady stream of meth. This dynamic was very common for the young people in my study. Most of the girls in my study identify boys and men as major contributors to their drug addiction.

A breakup with an intimate partner is another circumstance that can influence young women's use of drugs. Although such partners often contribute to girls' drug use, they can also provide emotional support to the girls while they deal with their turbulent home lives. For example, when Feliz's boyfriend Edwin cheated on her, it devastated her emotional well-being. For Feliz, her partner had become her principal motivation for doing well in school and her main emotional outlet while dealing with her unstable home life. She soon became depressed.

Several weeks later, Feliz's sister, Tiffany, noticed Feliz's depression and invited her to "hang out" with her and her friends. Two years older than Feliz, Tiffany was a sophomore in high school. Feliz began spending more time with Tiffany and her high school friends as she dealt with her grief. During this time, her sister began to comment on Feliz's depression. Tiffany and her friends were genuinely concerned about Feliz, so they tried to cheer her up by inviting her to smoke marijuana with the group. Before this invitation, Feliz had no idea her sister participated in this behavior. Feliz smoked marijuana for the first time and confided in Tiffany and her new friends about her recent breakup. Hearing this, her sister suddenly understood Feliz's new behavior. Tiffany said, "We don't wanna see you sad. We wanna see you happy."

Tiffany's response to this information was to introduce her sister to meth. That same day, she brought Feliz to a private room in her friend's house, where Feliz smoked methamphetamine for the first time. She described her experience to me:

> So they brought a pipe and crystal meth. They said, "Here, we have something for you." I was like, "What the fuck is that?" They're like, "Just take a hit. Take a hit, don't inhale, keep it in your mouth, and then blow out." I did it . . . and I felt amazing, you know? . . . I closed my eyes, and all of sudden chills went all throughout my body. [*Pause.*] I dunno, I just felt really good, and it made me instantly . . . have a different attitude. . . . I wasn't crying anymore. I felt like someone came in and replaced my emotions.

When first offered methamphetamine, Feliz was unfamiliar with it, and certainly didn't know how to ingest it. With instructions from her sister, she smoked for the first time. New meth users, like new marijuana users, often need someone to guide their first experience (Becker, 1953). However, unlike in the case of marijuana use, in which individuals learn how to interpret the effects of the drug from those around them, Feliz instantaneously identified the impact of methamphetamine on her mind. The "amazing" feeling was the release of endorphins into the brain triggered by ingesting this particular substance. Users of this drug describe this as an instantaneously "happy" feeling. Feliz experienced this same sensation and immediately shed her prolonged fight with depression. Meth and her new acquaintances provided her with a temporary avenue to escape her dejected state.

What Feliz did not realize is that meth is extremely addictive and expensive (U.S. Department of Justice, 2003). As is the case with most stimulants, users need to increase their consumption of the drug to continue experiencing the same effects that they did at the beginning. Feliz, like Ray, Maria, Sandra, Virginia, Aracely, and the other girls in my study, battled with drug addiction. And when their parents or guardians realized they were using drugs, these girls often suffered further abuse at home. Given these experiences, the girls in my study more often than not decided to run away from home.

RUNNING AWAY AND TROUBLE ON THE STREETS

Most scholarship on girls who run away establishes a clear pattern. Girls run away to avoid the trauma of living at home. We know that running away can expose girls to several added forms of interpersonal and sexual violence (Winn, 2011; Chesney-Lind and Shelden, 2014; Schaffner, 1998). We know less, however, about the strategies that girls employ to survive life on the streets. Most of the girls in my study chose one of two options when they decided to leave home: they moved in with an intimate partner, or they lived on the streets.[2] These decisions exposed the young women to more forms of gendered, socioeconomic, and racialized violence.

Living with a Romantic Partner

The young women in my study often moved in with their romantic partners to escape the abuse they experienced at home. After being forced to give up her child, twelve-year-old Debby wanted to be away from her violent family. Given this, she decided to move in with the father of her child after he returned to the United States. When she first moved in with him, things were going well. He would leave during the day to work, and she would stay home and take care of household duties. Debby was content with this traditional division of labor, but shortly after she moved in Daniel began cheating on her. He also began accusing Debby of infidelity. One day when she came home after school, she found him sleeping with another woman. She said, "I just thought it was like a fairy tale. Run away with him and then you have a picture perfect family. . . . [Instead] he just started freaking [sleeping with] other *heinas* [women]; and I still didn't leave him, *porque* [because] I was trying to get away from my mom."

Debby describes the predicament of countless young women who run away. First, they leave home to escape abuse. Many of them move in with their partners, only to see them become unfaithful, unstable, and abusive. While Daniel paid rent and bought Debby "everything," he also expected sex on demand and domestic work in return. As she continued to refuse Daniel's sexual advances, he became more abusive. "It was getting pretty bad; my next door neighbor, he would like hear me yell 'cause I was getting beat, beat bad." Keep in mind that Debby was a twelve-year-old, sixth-grade elementary school student at the time. Despite these challenges, she still attempted to attend school regularly.

Debby's semiregular presence at school begins to illustrate the short-comings of wraparound services, which are intended to help youth in multiple sites, including home and school. Debby did not receive any type of help until she was arrested and placed on formal probation. Once incarcerated and, later, on probation, she regularly received visits from probation officers and school resource officers, and she received therapeutic counseling behind bars, but before that, no social workers appeared to ask how she had become pregnant at eleven or why she was living with an adult man to whom she was not related. We can see that, at this point in Debby's life, she could have benefited tremendously from support at home or in school. But those services were not forthcoming. As is so often the case, wraparound services came too late to help but were quick to provide punishment. Eventually, Debby left Daniel permanently and returned to her mother's home.

Debby, like other young women with few resources, was sucked into what Anderson refers to as the "Game and the Dream" (1999, 151). This "dream" includes getting married, having children, finding stable employment, and moving into a safe neighborhood where one can raise a family. This is a desire to live a traditional American middle-class life, an experience most of the girls in my study never attained. The lure of this potential life often pulls girls into the "game," which refers to unhealthy living situations like the one Debby found herself in. The other young women who moved in with their partners all had similar experiences. Their initial expectations of a fairytale life away from home ended shortly after they moved in with their partners.

Living on the Streets

When girls have exhausted all their other resources, having tried staying with friends, extended families, or intimate partners, they are forced to live on the streets. Living on the streets exposes girls to forms of abuse that often includes sexual exploitation (Winn, 2011; Chesney-Lind and Shelden, 2014; Schaffner, 1998). To gain money for food and shelter, the young women in my study were often forced to shoplift, sell stolen goods, break into homes, or rob individuals. Some of the young women I spoke with were forced to work as "bait" for robberies and stickups that were perpetrated by men in their neighborhoods. Others turned to sex work to feed themselves and their drug addictions. While participating in sex work was a less common theme among the girls in my study, many found themselves sexually exploited.

Even those girls who were able to avoid sexual exploitation faced the constant threat of sexual abuse while navigating the street. Consider Amber. Amber lacked a deep network of friends when her mother kicked her out of the house, and so she found herself living on the streets. Amber is a seventeen-year-old, first-generation, self-identified Chicana. She had a auburn complexion and strong indigenous facial features. She looked tired and worn down when she nervously agreed to speak with me during an interview. She had left home at sixteen and begun working in the sex trade to support herself and her meth addiction.

During our interview at El Valle she went into gruesome detail about the challenges of sex work and living on the streets. She also described the process of how she ended up working in this field in the first place. She recalled how her mother "*me corrió* [ran me out]. . . . I started hustling, . . . and then I got my own little job. I became independent." This pattern is very common for underage girls who participate in the sex economy (Horning, 2013; Dank, 2011; Van Brunschot and Brannigan, 2002). In her eyes, sex work allowed her to be independent and self-reliant, a factor that commonly pulls girls into this line of work (Horning, 2013; Dank, 2011; Van Brunschot and Brannigan, 2002). But Amber also had no alternative but to be self-reliant, since she had few friends, no partner, and even fewer resources. She explained,

> Let me ask you: . . . *Tu que harías en la calle?* [What would you do on the street?] *Ponte a pensar que haces cuando no tienes comida.* [Think about what you would do if you had no food.] *Comó Chicana? Ponte a pensar Guey.* [Think about it from my point of view as a Chicana.] What do you do if the landlord says, "You need to pay me rent right now"? Let's say you have an interview. You can go to the interview and see if they might hire you? Even if your stuff might be outside in the street when you get back home? . . . Or are you going to go to the homey that says, "I can help you make two thousand dollars right now"? . . . You take the two thousand dollars because it's a sure thing.

Away from home and on the street, she began to work in the underground sex economy because she felt it was her only resource. Hustling would put a roof over her head and food in her mouth, and would allow her to feed her increasing drug dependence. Given that she lacked a high school education, special training, and any kind of family support, sex work seemed like a reasonable decision compared to the possibility of a job in the formal sector. Thus, she continued to work in the sex trade. The more time she spent doing so, the more drugs she consumed to deal with the trauma of this harsh profession.

Amber's story speaks to the experiences of a majority of the girls in my study. Although their hustling did not always entail formal sex work, their friends, family, and people on the street often used their bodies and sexuality for their own benefit. For example, young women like Aracely were encouraged to use their sexuality to aid older men in the community with robberies. Older men in the neighborhood often asked her to serve as "bait" for robberies by walking down the street and convincing a potential target that she was interested in sexual intercourse. She said, "Me and this girl, we went out, [and] people stopped in their car. . . . They wanted to pick us up. . . . Once we got to their house, one of us comes out and starts walking down the street; and all of the sudden, you just see the homeys [older men] rush in." This is only one of the various ways that young women are encouraged to use their sexuality to help men in their neighborhood. In other instances, young women living on the streets help get targets for gang retaliation drunk to make them more susceptible targets. Other girls are encouraged to have sex with friends, acquaintances, and family members in exchange for drugs or a place to stay. The young women in my study could not escape the constant threat of sexual coercion and exploitation once on the street.

All of the girls in my study ran away from home at least once before coming to El Valle. While some left for a weekend or a few nights, others stayed away for extended periods or were kicked out by their parents. For most of the participants in my study, being on the streets resulted in increased drug addiction. The addictions they developed on the street adversely impacted the rest of their young lives. It is also important to note that, when girls ran away, they seldom attended school—a choice that exposed them to the possibility of arrest for truancy. This finding is consistent with research that shows how girls' survival strategies are criminalized (Chesney-Lind and Shelden, 2014; Schaffner, 1998). The girls often experienced their first arrest and booking into El Valle Juvenile Detention Facility either while living on the streets or shortly after they returned home. Table 2 in appendix 2 has information about my research participants' age of first arrest and the location where this took place.

FIRST CONTACT WITH THE CRIMINAL JUSTICE SYSTEM

The young women in my study were first arrested at home, in school, or on the street. But no matter where they were at the moment of their arrest, their experiences at home ultimately led to their eventual incarceration. Those troubles were directly connected to the girls' initially being caught up by the criminal justice system.

An overwhelming proportion of the girls in my study were arrested on the street. Some were arrested for truancy, running away, being under the influence, or being in possession of a controlled substance. A small number were arrested for fighting. The most common cause for arrest on the streets, however, was girls' participation in drug use. Their involvement in these nonviolent crimes was directly connected to the time they spend on the street, whether they ran away from home or were kicked out by their parents. Maria, for example, said, "I think I started coming here [to the detention center] when I was fifteen and a half; I got caught shoplifting." While Maria had somewhere to stay when she left her family's home, she did not have access to clothes and self-care products. Given this, she decided to shoplift, was caught, and was subsequently incarcerated. Similarly, Sandra broke into a stranger's home with a group of friends because "we needed the money." They collectively robbed the home, and she attempted to sell the stolen goods at a local pawnshop. The owner notified the police, who soon arrived at the location where she was staying. Her adult friends convinced her to take the fall for the crime since she was underage and would receive only a short time behind bars. A small group of the girls in my study were arrested for strong-arm robbery. While this group was extremely small, it is important to note that this type of crime too, which was associated with the need for cash on the street, led to girls' first arrest and incarceration.

Fewer than a quarter of my participants were arrested for the first time at home or school. Those who were arrested in the home fell into two other categories. First, some girls were arrested for fighting with their parents. These cases involved girls physically fighting back against abuse or their parents' attempts to physically beat or restrain them. The parents, however, were usually not arrested during these altercations. It is important to note that some of these incidents began after parents had kicked their children out of the house. Some of these youth attempted to return home, only to encounter hostile parents who did not want them back. In these cases, parents often fought with their children in an attempt to get them to leave their homes. Second, some girls were arrested after their parents found they were under the influence of or had possession of a controlled substance. In these situations, parents called the police, with the result that the girls were arrested and taken to El Valle Juvenile Detention Facility.

It was extremely rare for a girl to experience her first arrest at school. The few young women who were initially detained at school were arrested either for being under the influence or for an incident related to problems in their homes. The rarity of this event is probably explained by the fact that girls who leave home rarely attend school. The criminal justice system mandates that, once incarcerated, however, young people must attend school, and so missing school is considered a criminal offense, a probation violation, and an action worthy of more time behind bars. Once on probation, the young women in my study were regularly arrested on campus or for not attending school. For the girls in my study, increased surveillance in the form of formal probation resulted in more sanctions at home, at school, in the community, and behind bars. This probation was a key component of wraparound services, which regularly resulted in girls spending more time in El Valle.

When arrested for the first time, the girls were taken to secure detention, placed on formal probation, and often taken to a group home upon their release. Once connected to the criminal justice system, the girls often remained linked to this system for most of their adolescence.

ELECTRONIC MONITORING AND PLACEMENT

After their first visit to El Valle, most of the girls left with an electronic monitoring anklet, a circumstance commonly known as "house arrest" or "EM." This around-the-clock, hands-off monitoring technique—a central component of wraparound services—allows law enforcement agents to pinpoint individuals' exact whereabouts at all times. The anklet can also signal agents if or when a youth removes it. This approach to surveillance is supposed to save local law enforcement agencies money, since it is substantially cheaper than housing youth in the detention center. Given the relatively low cost of this supervision, the probation department often allows youths to finish a portion of their sentences on EM instead of serving their whole jail terms in El Valle. Others are required to be on EM as a part of their formal probation. Having been fitted with this tracking device, the young women return either to their own homes or to a supervised group home.

While EM is an effective cost-cutting strategy, most of the girls in my study did not do well on house arrest. In fact, almost all the participants in my study were rearrested when released on house arrest. The explanation is predictable and obvious: Their home life was still unsafe and almost always unstable. The same factors that contributed to girls' initial troubles with the law reappeared when they returned home on EM. In addition, the girls in my study found it difficult to remain sober when returned to their originating community. Given that most of the girls in my research were arrested for drug charges, this last factor is extremely important. Most of the girls I spoke with cut off their anklets and ran away multiple times. Once they left home, they experienced the same challenges and participated in the same high-risk behavior they had engaged in previously. For these youth, house arrest was too good to be true: the combination of an adverse home environment and the ability to walk out the door at any time was too tempting. This often led to extended periods on the street, more time on formal probation, and eventually more time in El Valle Juvenile Detention Facility, and it demonstrates another shortcoming of wraparound services.

The circumstances surrounding the rearrest of girls in "placement" requires more explanation. *Placement* is a phrase commonly used by youth to refer to any form of living in the foster care system. Almost all the young women in my study had lived in a group home, or "placement," at least once during their young lives. A handful first entered placement when city or school officials realized they were being abused in their own homes. For most of my participants, however, their first exposure to placement homes came after their release from juvenile detention. Indeed, some girls were required to remain at El Valle after their formal release date while administrators attempted to find them a placement home.

Depending on a girl's original circumstances, a placement home might or might not represent an improvement. A number of studies have found that placement homes often expose girls to potential threats of violence (Jones, 2010). For example, researchers have documented that child abuse and neglect are often an intimate part of life inside group homes in the United States and Canada (Chesney-Lind and Shelden, 2014). In an ethnographic study of a Canadian group home, Brown (2010) found that girls constantly worried about potential threats of violence, both from other residents and from staff members. Furthermore, Crosland and colleagues (2008) found that staff members in American group homes are often ill-equipped and undertrained to deal with potential threats, further exacerbating potentially volatile interactions. This research is consistent with my own findings.

The young women in my study believed that "placement is just like being locked up." Placement exposed them to forms of surveillance similar to those in secure detention. For example, there were often cameras, random searches by placement staff, and drug tests. My study participants also complained that staff members treated them poorly and instigated fights to get girls they didn't like kicked out of the placement home. For girls on probation, getting kicked out of a placement home meant another jail sentence. Other girls had to navigate threats of interpersonal violence similar to those they had encountered on the street. They were often exposed to other young women who were more than eager to fight; with the girls' ready access to kitchen knives and other household items, these fights had the potential to inflict serious injury. Like getting kicked out, a fight in placement resulted in more time in detention.

Leaving placement was a temptation most youth could not resist. As Ray explained, "It sucks. It's tempting to walk out, because you have that ability. You're scared to walk out. You can walk out, but if you do you're in trouble, you're a runaway." Ray and many of the other girls decided to run away from placement homes; however, once on the street they followed the same familiar patterns. Because they receive little therapy or other services to address their prior abuse, psychological trauma, and drug addiction, it is no surprise that most of these young women relapse into criminal behavior on multiple occasions. On average, the girls in my study were incarcerated on seven separate occasions, and some were arrested as many as nineteen times. Once they were on probation, any slipup resulted in a visit to secure detention. The pattern of surveillance, interpersonal violence, and punishment was ubiquitous in the lives of girls in my study. Taken as a whole, these events led the girls to become caught up in the criminal justice system.

CHAPTER 2

Life behind Bars

Alexis looks as if she hasn't slept in days. We sit in the five-by-five-foot cinder-block room in the detention center and talk. The correctional officers cannot hear us, but they can watch us from a small viewing window above. They periodically peer down as Alexis tells me why she decided to assault three fellow inmates after one of them made what she considered to be racist remarks in class:

> You know how people say, "Think about the consequences—you don't think about the consequences before you act"? And I really do. I will sit there and debate with myself: this is what will happen if you fight, and this is what will happen if you don't. And I had already let them slide too many times. She would have kept on acting up and trying to step all over me. And it's about reputation. To me it's like a dent in my reputation. . . . I felt like she was extremely racist and justice had to be served.

Alexis gives us a look inside the thoughts and rationale of someone who is deciding whether to fight another inmate in El Valle Juvenile Detention Facility. Contrary to staff members' belief—that girls fight because they lack self-restraint or are "just bad"—Alexis considers various components of a thought process when making her decision. After a quick cost-benefit analysis, she decides to invest in a fight regardless of the physical and administrative consequences. In her case, she received a seventy-two-hour "Do not release from cell" order, added jail time, and a transfer to the maximum security unit. Alexis felt she needed to put a stop to this girl's behavior even though she was aware of the probable consequences. "Justice," in her eyes, needed "to be served." For Alexis, fighting is not simply about physically attacking someone; it's about sending a message to other girls *and staff* that she is not to be disrespected.

In this and other American detention centers, violence is ubiquitous, a central part of life behind bars (Flores, 2013; Bickel, 2010). Most research in this area focuses on the violence that takes place among fellow inmates (Davis, 2003). These studies often find that incarcerated individuals cannot escape fighting, even when they expressly desire to avoid this behavior (Burton-Rose, 2003). My findings from my time spent observing the girls at El Valle suggest that the behavior of the correctional staff contributes to fighting and other forms of violence in secure detention. The institution and its staff both promote problematic behaviors (like fighting) and create an atmosphere where these behaviors are necessary. Encouraging such behaviors might help keep girls safe in detention, but it ultimately further entrenches these young women in the El Valle-Legacy Community School cycle and the larger criminal justice system, contrary to the stated goals of the institutions that promote wraparound services. Most of the young people in this study were initially arrested for nonviolent, drug-related offenses, but they earned additional time in secure confinement because of fighting. In other words, girls began participating in violent behavior *after* entering El Valle Juvenile Detention Facility.

THE ROLE OF FIGHTING IN MAINTAINING TOTAL CONTROL

At El Valle, young women's bodies and behaviors are constrained and policed in many ways. All the girls receive a wake-up call through the intercom in their standard, single-bed, gray cell at 6:15 A.M. Officers instruct them to prepare their things for a mandatory shower at 6:30; each girl is permitted five minutes to shower in a communal bathroom. After this, they are escorted back into their cells, which the girls refer to as "going down" or "taking it down." At 7, they are escorted into the day room, where they receive breakfast, which consists of oatmeal, a piece of fruit, and a carton of milk. The girls are given twenty minutes to eat, then are escorted back into their cells. Between 8 and 8:30, they are guided into classrooms. School operates on a schedule of one-and-a-half-hour blocks. The girls spend one block of time with one math/science teacher, followed by another block with one English/history teacher. After each block, the teachers rotate from House One to House Two, or the reverse. Students do not come in contact with girls from the opposite houses. This schedule runs from 8:30 A.M. to 2:50 P.M., Monday through Friday. Between each block, the girls must line up and be searched by correctional officers, after which they receive a thirty-minute break, snack, or lunch. When the school day ends, the girls are ushered into the exercise yard for one hour of semiorganized physical activity, such as light stretching or a game of basketball or kickball.

Once girls return inside, they are searched again, and from 4 to 5 P.M. all of the girls participate in programming that usually includes anger management, sex education, or money management skills. Once they leave the programming, they are searched yet again and taken into their cells, where they stay from 5 to 6 P.M. Finally, they are allowed two hours of free time to eat dinner, watch a television located in the day room, converse with their friends in a low voice, read, or play board games. At 8 P.M. they are given medication (if needed) and searched yet again, and they take it down for the last time. Any violations of this schedule result in institutional sanctions, including restrictions on free time, a ban on watching television or listening to the radio, a twenty-four-hour isolation order, or a trip to the maximum-security unit of the facility. Youth can also be pepper-sprayed or fined for violating this schedule. Most severely, they can have days added to their terms of incarceration. In this space, girls' behavior is constantly regimented, surveilled, disciplined, and controlled. But despite living under conditions of hypersurveillance, girls at El Valle fight regularly.

Encouraging Fighting

At El Valle, and other institutions of confinement, correctional officers are charged with maintaining the safety of people in their facility (Dvoskin and Spiers, 2004). The California youth correctional officer manual states that an officer "assists in maintaining total facility security and safety [and] . . . establishes rapport and communicates with youthful offenders on a daily basis" (California Department of Corrections and Rehabilitation, 1998). This often means that officers are almost completely consumed with maintaining order and punishing youths who violate this order.

Although it may seem counterintuitive, encouraging girls to fight can aid the correctional officers in their search for social control. The detained girls at El Valle pick up on this; during my time at the facility, I observed how developing a reputation as a fighter or a "shot caller" could be protective. Shot callers are ready and willing to fight at the slightest sign of disrespect. Correctional officers are less likely to punish shot callers and are more cautious when interacting with them than with nonfighters. They are also less likely to physically or verbally abuse fighters, and they avoid antagonizing them. Conversely, not fighting earns girls the opposite treatment by jail staff.

During a recent "riot," several girls organized four fights that took place simultaneously. Feliz, whom I introduced in the previous chapter, told me about the event during an interview. She also explained how her interactions with correctional officers changed for the better after this incident.

> After the riot a lot of CSOs [Corrections Service officers] came up to tell me that they watched the videos of our fight, or my fight. It was crazy, like hearing them say that was cool. You know? Now the new CSOs know me; [they're] like, "Oh, there's that crazy girl." It's just like knowing that they know what you can do. . . . It feels good to us. It feels good to me. . . . [Now] they're more kick back [relaxed] with me, actually. . . . They shake hands and shit. . . . It is weird. It's all, like, they respected it. . . . For some reason it seems like they liked it. It was their entertainment. 'Cause even when I was seg'd [segregated], a lot of CSOs would be bringing me snacks and stuff. It was just different. . . . It felt good.

As a result of this fighting, Feliz was placed in the maximum-security unit of the facility, located in a secluded part of the detention center. But instead of punishing her, the correctional officers stopped by to congratulate her, making her feel special on account of her display of violence. Reflecting on these events, Feliz says that this new special treatment and respect "felt good." Despite the institutional sanctions she received, Feliz has no motivation to stop fighting. Ironically, officers undermined the punishment (segregation) they themselves imposed by valorizing the behavior. In doing so, officers helped promote violence and reified the girl's reputation as a fighter. By rewarding Feliz for these actions, correctional officers encouraged her to participate in this behavior again. This can also send signals to other girls at the facility, letting them know that fighting is something they should seek to accomplish.

How Correctional Staff Use Reputations as Currency
During a visit to the facility, I was sitting in the day room, where the gray walls of the facility and the waxed floors have a sanitized feel. The light musty odor that hangs in the air reminds me of a locker room in a gym. As I sit, I hear Crystal, a sixteen-year-old, say, "He is not even your man. I don't know why you are making such a big deal about it." Rain, a year younger, replies, "Yeah, he is bitch!" She starts to punch Crystal, who is sitting in a gray love seat. Crystal leans back, places her right leg on Rain's chest and holds her away from her body. A correctional officer yells, "Drop!" and the other girls hit the waxed floor as Crystal and Rain continue their exchange. The officer jogs over to the girls and pulls Rain by the hair onto the floor. One officer commands her to "stop moving" as she places handcuffs on her. This staff member outweighs Rain by approximately a hundred pounds. The officer then places her knee on Rain's back and orders the other girls to their cells. Simultaneously, five other correctional officers enter the girls' unit, and three of them escort Rain to her cell. After the students are back in their cells, the officer who pulled Rain by the hair turns to me and another instructor and says, "I should have sprayed them [Crystal and Rain] so we could have kept them in their rooms for the rest of the day." By "spray," she is referring to oleoresin capsicum, popularly known as "pepper spray." Correctional officers use this when girls fight or refuse to follow their orders.

The officer's comments provide some insight into how and why staff use fights to achieve social order and control. Had she sprayed the two girls, she could have kept all of them in their rooms all day, away from school. This would have made the officers' jobs substantially easier, since it would not have been necessary to check the classrooms every fifteen minutes, escort the girls to other classes, or search them afterward. When the girls remain in their cells, officers can simply relax, read, listen to the radio, or watch television; I have seen this process take place during my fieldwork. For example, one day I saw one of the officers spray a student with pepper spray. She ordered the unit to return to their cells, even though class was supposed to be in session. She said, "I think school is going to be cancelled for the rest of the day." The girls were in their rooms for twenty minutes while she called her supervisor to tell her the news. Fifteen minutes later, the supervisor returned to the unit, saying, "We need to send them to school if we want to or not. California law requires it." The officer let out a "damn it" before instructing the girls to return to class.

Correctional officers are not the only El Valle staff to benefit from fighting. On one visit to the detention center, I was speaking to a teacher during a break. As we sat in her classroom, we discussed some of the "fighters" at the facility. During our conversation, she noted, "I like to make friends with the fighters, because the other girls listen to them and it makes controlling the class easier. They help keep the other girls in check." Ms. Sanchez would befriend these students by asking them to help her with tasks around the classroom, by speaking to them before and after class, and by rewarding them with snacks and songs on the radio. Although Ms. Sanchez did this with other girls as well, she intentionally targeted students with reputations as fighters.

Ms. Sanchez provides the most cogent and convincing example of correctional staff using girls' reputations to achieve their own goals. The teacher shifts partial responsibility for order onto certain adolescents instead of maintaining it herself. Previous ethnographic research on classroom management in the United States shows that most teachers either stop class to speak to a disruptive student, or simply ask them to leave the classroom (Hurd, 2004). Here, Ms. Sanchez uses an alternative strategy that has worked during her tenure at the facility. Using this technique allows her to avoid classroom management techniques that cause larger disruptions. But by not taking full responsibility for classroom management, she assigns part of this duty to students who can and will impose their will on other girls.

Teaching in correctional facilities in the United States can be challenging: students can have untreated disabilities, may be detoxifying or intoxicated, and may not have attended school regularly for most of their lives (Zabel and Nigro, 2007). Ms. Sanchez co-opts "fighters" because it makes her job easier. When the class gets out of hand, for example, the fighters help calm and control the rest of the students by telling them to "stop talking" or "shut up." If students disrespect Ms. Sanchez, these girls will speak up and say, "Hey, you need to stop that. Now!" Because of their fierce reputation, other students are more likely to listen to them for fear of retaliation. It is unclear if the girls fully understand what is taking place; it was not clear to me whether the fighters participate in this behavior because it gives them an opportunity to exercise their power, or because the added attention they receive from the teacher makes them feel special. Either way, however, this practice simultaneously reifies these girls' reputations as fighters and promotes violence in what is supposed to be a recuperative space. Ms. Sanchez is a kind and dedicated teacher, but in embracing this approach she is complicit in re-creating the power dynamics that encourage violence and contribute to girls spending more time behind bars.

This re-creation of power dynamics can occur consciously and subconsciously. I had a similar experience during a poetry workshop I was teaching in the unit. I was trying to quiet the class, when one of the girls said "shut up!" and laughed out loud. Ray turned to the girl who said this and took her to task, saying, "Hey! You don't talk like that to him!" After this statement, the girl stopped laughing and the rest of the students lowered their voices. At the time that this exchange took place, I had not yet discerned what was happening; I did not understand how I had become complicit in re-creating and benefiting from the girls' reputations. My failure to stop this behavior helped Ray reassert her status and power at the facility. The process of re-creating dysfunctional power dynamics is not always premeditated.

In other cases, the correctional officers seemed to be using the threat of fights to discipline the girls. At one point while conducting fieldwork, I overheard a correctional officer say to a student, "Keep that attitude up. Someone is going to beat your ass one day, and you have it coming! You have a bad attitude, and someone is going to get tired of it one day!" This incident surprised me. It was the first time I had heard such an explicit threat, and I wondered if this was more than just a scolding. Did the threat carry more weight because it was delivered in front of the other girls and staff?

Wanting to find out more, I asked Crystal about fighting at the facility:

CRYSTAL: Usually staff here, they'll let you get down [fight]. And when they call it in, that's when they break it up. Some staff do that.

JERRY: So, they'll let you fight?

CRYSTAL: Uh-huh.

JERRY: Why do you think they do that? To let you get it out?

CRYSTAL: Yeah, because, it's 'cause staff doesn't like the girl either. I don't know—if she's really annoying or she complains too much. And they don't like that. They don't like that, they don't like people like that.

According to Crystal, officers don't like girls who complain or girls who are "annoying." As a form of reprisal for their problematic behavior, officers will let them fight instead of intervening immediately. They do this by being slow to respond to a dispute, or by calling for backup before they attempt to stop the incident. When the girls heard the correctional officer threaten that someday a student would get beaten up, they knew the guards would not rush to her defense if someone attacked her. This example embodies the narratives of the rest of the girls I interviewed.

All girls, fighters or nonfighters, understand that correctional staff can stop fights or choose to let them happen. They are also aware of the contingent nature of their safety, and that only they can keep themselves safe in El Valle. Some girls achieve this by fighting or developing a reputation as someone who will fight if challenged, even though this strategy earns them more time behind bars. However, both fighting and not fighting are strategies that require investing time and effort.

CHOOSING TO FIGHT

Feliz first arrived at El Valle when she was fifteen years old. She recalled her first experience of entering the facility: "One of the older girls [Aracely] came up to me and was like, 'Where are you from?' I said, 'Nowhere, but do you have a problem?' The older girl laughed and said, 'Nah, foo. Come kick it with us.'" This initial encounter with Aracely was more than an informal greeting and neighborhood/gang affiliation check. This conversation was the first part of a complex initiation process. Unfamiliar with these dynamics, Feliz befriended Aracely, who over the course of six years had established a reputation among youth and jail staff as a shot caller. Few girls or even jail staff contest Aracely's authority at El Valle. To establish her dominance, Aracely and her close-knit group of friends participate in planned and predetermined behavior that reinforces their identities.

When Feliz approached Aracely about getting initiated into the shot caller group, Aracely and the other two members decided to plan a "riot." These actions involved fighting multiple girls simultaneously at a predetermined date and time. For the girls in the facility, planning a riot would serve multiple purposes. For example, it would prove to the other shot callers that Feliz was willing to protect the group against physical or symbolic challenges. Although Feliz knew she would likely be punished and earn more time in detention for fighting, she understood that fighting is necessary in this space. She saw it as a rite of passage that demonstrated her commitment to the other shot callers. Planning a riot would be Feliz's ticket to status, power, and protection in the facility. Feliz recalls, "Basically, they were trying to name me, so they're like, '[If] you wanna show us that you're someone, to get a name, go do something.'" And I was like, 'All right.' So we planned out a riot. We let one of the girls who was nothing into it to start it [the riot], 'cause we didn't wanna get caught for starting it. We just wanted to be a part of it. And she ratted on us." When the new girl told jail staff what was being planned, the group was infuriated. Now, the riot had two goals: to initiate Feliz into the group and punish the girl who told the authorities about their plans. Making an example of the "rat" would send a message to the other girls that violating their authority would not be tolerated.

Although some of the staff suspected something was going on, they largely believed rumors about a "riot" to be merely gossip. Feliz remembers starting the fight: "We had a reason to fight her, so I went up to her and was like, 'Get up.' And I started socking her, and all of sudden two of the girls came up right behind me and started socking her with me, and everyone went crazy after that." While Feliz and the other shot callers pummeled the youth who had told the authorities about the riot, the other girls in the unit followed instructions they had been given earlier. One girl sprayed shampoo and lotion on the floor, causing the correctional guards to slip when they attempted to intervene. As the three girls continued to pummel the fourth, another managed to wrestle away a correctional officer's pepper spray. She then sprayed the guards and the other girls who did not participate. Other girls started banging their lunch trays against the tables; those who were still in their rooms pushed their mattresses against their cell doors. It took fifteen officers entering the unit to eventually stop the riot. The officers removed the main participants from the unit and placed them in a separate, temporary holding cell.

Feliz, as we have seen, was sent to the maximum-security unit as part of her punishment for starting the fight, where the staff rewarded her behavior. When she returned to the main unit, she found that the other young women, too, treated her differently. She said that one of the major changes was that girls "respected" her more than they had in the past. Now young women ask her for advice and for her opinion on issues in detention and in the community. They also consult Feliz about how to navigate life in El Valle. "It's like we are celebrities. And our reputation is being fearless. We're not gonna let you hurt me or bother us. And I'm gonna make you feel this way because I have the power." Most importantly, girls seem afraid and cautious around her. Feliz said, "People act different when they know you have someone on your side. You feel invincible when you do have that." Instead of feeling vulnerable, she feels "invincible." These changes have improved her standard of living in El Valle, despite having earned her more time there.

Despite being punished, Feliz says the riot "was worth it" because it completed her initiation into the shot caller group. She demonstrated that she was willing and able to physically enforce the repercussions of defying the group. She also demonstrated to the correctional staff and other inmates that she is not to be taken lightly. In the context of this study, the use of violence is premeditated, not situational (Jones, 2010; Randall, 2008; Anderson, 1999). It manifests as a planned set of actions with an intended set of goals. These actions also have adverse consequences; but for girls like Feliz, fighting provides long-term benefits that outweigh the short-term discomforts.

Reputation Management

Fighting in El Valle is a key component of gaining favorable treatment from other girls and staff. At the same time, the shot callers and any others who fight must walk a fine line between fighting and following the rules, including attending school, not complaining, and not overtly disrespecting jail staff. Not following the rules might result in staff withdrawing their support, in spite of a girl's reputation as a shot caller. Although youth at El Valle might not tolerate disrespect from other girls, they know they must respect the institutional actors. Not doing so could inadvertently prolong their sentences or result in the loss of privileges. Bonita is a seventeen-year-old, middle-class young Latina woman who started coming to the facility when she was fourteen. She discussed the need to respect the staff:

> BONITA: Yeah, respect is gained, you know; but at the same time you do have to give it to get it.
>
> JERRY: So, how do you get respect?
>
> BONITA: By just doing what you are supposed to be doing, working your program, not trying to fight all the time. . . . Just behaving. . . .
>
> JERRY: So, what do you mean by "working your program"?
>
> BONITA: Don't talk back to the staff, work with the nonprofit program, go to school, don't refuse [staff's orders]. [Don't say,] "Oh, I am not gonna do my math" . . . if you go to class.

Bonita adds another layer of understanding to this complex interaction. While jail staff give kudos to girls who fight, provide them with snacks, and rarely disrespect them, they can also take away their privileges. Youth can lose privileges, even unofficial privileges, by not "working [the] program," as Bonita mentioned. Overt disrespect of the staff and disregard for the basic rules are usually met with punishment, both officially, in the form of a do-not-release order or a lengthier sentence, and informally, through the loss of snacks and entertainment privileges. Fighting provides long-term benefits that outweigh the short-term punishments, but the choice to fight also depends on walking the fine line between breaking and obeying the rules.

"I'll Give 'em a Fight"

Unlike the shot callers, some of the girls at El Valle fight only if necessary. For the most part, these individuals attempt to avoid fighting. They do not challenge people and try to stay away from circumstances that might spur confrontation. They know that not standing up for oneself results in disrespect and punishment from inmates and staff.

One of the strategies these girls use to avoid fighting is "talking it out." Sometimes disputes at the jail occur despite efforts to avoid gossip and negative interactions. When this occurs, some girls are able to discuss the issue that is bothering them without getting involved in a physical altercation.

Sixteen-year-old Mariana is a second-generation Latina with a copper complexion and dark hair. She describes how some individuals talk it out:

> Sometimes if the person is mature, they will talk about it; and it is also depending on what it is. . . . Sometimes they will just talk about it and get their stories straight, and that is what I did. . . . I went to beat this girl up because this [other] girl was telling me things. . . . So I asked her, "What is really going on?" And she told me a whole different story from the one my friend told me. And I know my friend lies. Sometimes it is good to talk it out, because you don't know.

Once Mariana compared stories with the other girl, they discovered that a mutual acquaintance was creating rumors; this wasn't something worth fighting about. At the same time, Mariana understands that you cannot talk it out with everyone. The girl must be willing to listen to what you have to say.

Annabelle is a slender, light-skinned Latina whose family was involved with a neighborhood gang. In El Valle, Annabelle had an issue with Christina, a girl from a rival neighborhood. She discussed how she talked out her problems with Christina and avoided a fight: "[I said,] 'Come here. Let's go take a walk. Let's talk about this. I wanna know what you're saying. If you have problems with me, we could fight. I have no problem. We could handle it, but after that I don't expect us to be like little girls and continuing it on with the "he said/she said" stuff.' We talked about it, and we squashed it, and she's actually one of my really close friends now." Most importantly, Annabelle demonstrated to her rival her willingness to fight. Showing a willingness to fight, even if the fight doesn't actually take place, maintains a girl's reputation.

While talking it out can help resolve issues, these interactions can be dangerous, because some girls who attempt to talk it out may have to fight despite their efforts to avoid a physical exchange. Nineteen-year-old Mary is five foot three, with a brown complexion. She, like many of the girls, has tattoos on her wrist and neck. Her approach to solving disputes is similar to Annabelle's. However, she also discussed the repercussions of fighting when trying to defuse a situation: "I tell girls it's not worth it. You're gonna get another charge. Then you're gonna get three months [added to your sentence]. I just tell 'em, 'You guys, it's really immature. Grow up.' . . . Then they sit and think about it." Mary is older than most of the other girls at El

Valle, having spent several years in and out of secure detention. She attempts to level with younger girls on the topic of fighting, in the hope that they will think twice about participating in this behavior.

In a separate incident, fifteen-year-old Sandra attempted to talk out a problem that occurred outside of detention. Sandra saw her boyfriend holding hands with and kissing another girl at a local fair. She said nothing that night, but she confronted this girl when she appeared at El Valle. "[I told her,] 'I seen you together at the fair,' and she denied it to me. She denied it to me. And . . . then my homegirl comes in [and says,] . . . 'Yeah, that's her.' And she lied to me. So then I told her, . . . 'You need to get down [fight],' and she's like, 'All right, then.'" If the other girl had admitted her actions, Sandra would have "let it go." Since she denied it, though, it ultimately resulted in a fight. While girls like Sandra attempt to talk out their problems, a fight is sometimes unavoidable.

THE RISKS OF NOT FIGHTING

For girls who cannot join the shot caller group and are not willing to fight, life in El Valle can become extremely isolating. Nevertheless, some youth here choose not to fight, avoid making friends, and spend most of their time in silence. They attempt to fly under the radar and hope that they can avoid random attacks. During my fieldwork, I observed that some of these girls often sat away from the group and seldom spoke. This interpersonal technique for avoiding violence resembles what Jones refers to as "relational isolation." Relational isolation "illuminates the work girls do to isolate themselves from close friendships, especially those with other young women. . . . By avoiding close friendships, girls can reduce the likelihood of their involvement in a physical conflict" (2010, 54). Similarly, girls at El Valle use this strategy to navigate the host of potential interpersonal and institutional forms of violence they may experience.

Fifteen-year-old Rasta is an energetic and outspoken white girl. At five foot eight, she is taller than most girls in the facility but has a lanky build. Rasta explained her place in El Valle during an interview:

I'm kind of at the bottom. I just kick it. Everyone likes me, but people still talk shit. . . . And then, let's see, well, Aracely [and other] people who have been here a really long time, they're kind of at the top. 'Cause if you say something, they fight you. . . . Like with Alexis: you know no one stands up to her, and it's really funny. No one corrects [her] reading if she makes a mistake [in class]. No one tells her nothing! But when I'm fucking reading and I make mistakes, that's a big, huge deal.

Rasta is aware that girls "talk shit" and tease her for several reasons. While she does not completely appreciate this taunting and disrespect, she understands the behavior to be relatively innocuous. Her status requires that she deal with this unwelcome behavior or fight. She contrasts her experience with that of Aracely and other girls, who are protected from the kinds of disrespect she receives regularly. Because Rasta chooses not to fight, she spends most of her time sitting quietly, writing in a journal, or sleeping in her cell.

During the research process, I heard the phrase "I just keep to myself" multiple times. I attempted to unravel the meaning of this expression and how girls deployed it as a strategy to avoid violence. Eighteen-year-old Destiny discussed how she approached life at El Valle: "[I say,] 'Just stick to yourself and go to a different table and read a book or play cards with yourself or something, or just go to your room and go to sleep.' . . . I don't care if those other girls respect me or disrespect me, I'm just gonna keep my mouth shut. . . . I try to stay away from that and not cause it [a fight] to happen. . . . 'Just stick to yourself and do what you gotta do and mind your own business.'" For the most part Destiny tries to avoid the other girls in the unit. She does this by spending time in her cell, playing solitaire, or just sitting quietly for extended periods. She does everything in her power to avoid a physical altercation. This includes staying quiet when someone is "talking shit" or when someone has wronged her. Unlike other girls in El Valle, Destiny is not particularly concerned with respect or disrespect. She knows that respect and a good reputation must be earned, and she is not willing to invest in that status. Instead, she avoids making friendships in the facility and mingling with other youth. Destiny is a good example of relational isolation in practice.

Making friends at El Valle is a risky endeavor. While acquaintances can potentially help win fights or assist with other difficult situations, befriending someone in El Valle can also expose a person to danger. The nonfighting girls I spoke with avoided friendships not only because they wanted to avoid commitments during difficult situations but also because they feared betrayal. I asked seventeen-year-old Bell, another of the few white girls in the facility, if she had any particular strategies for avoiding fights. She said, "A lot of the fights with some of the girls are started by just them getting to know other people and rumors getting spread. Like I said, I am not here to make friends and I don't care what people think. . . . I try not to give the girls a reason [to fight], you know? I don't talk about my life. I try to keep to myself." She does not speak about her life, because the answers can trigger fights about gang or neighborhood affiliation. She avoids making friends, because so-called friends might start rumors about her that could lead to a fight. Finally, she keeps to herself to avoid any confusion or misunderstandings that might lead to a potentially violent encounter. Like Destiny, Bell has little concern for her reputation: she cares little for earning respect from other youth.

Other girls, like sixteen-year-old Mari, even wanted to avoid discussing fights, rumors, and disputes between girls at El Valle. Mari said, "I don't like to ask them about their problems, 'cause then later on . . . I'll be involved in the problem." Avoiding certain people and certain topics of discussion allows the girls to decrease the chances they will be involved in a fight. But while using relational isolation helps in this setting, it does not ultimately guarantee safety. Despite this, several girls in the unit chose to keep to themselves to avoid potential conflicts.

Shannon, a seventeen-year-old white girl from a suburban community, discussed how isolating herself from other youth in the unit helped her avoid fighting. She also discussed how using relational isolation affected her emotional well-being: "I just don't stand up for myself, 'cause sometimes girls see me and say something to me, . . . and I will not do anything. . . . I'm by myself a lot here. . . . I feel lonely and bored 'cause I have none of my friends here, you know? I have no one to . . . have my back or hang out with. . . . It just kinda makes me sad when I think about [it]. . . . I'm alone and lonely." Shannon illustrates how relational isolation works at El Valle. While most other girls fight when insulted, she does not. She understands she is at a disadvantage because she does not have her friends from the community to support her during an altercation. While using relational isolation can help keep girls safe, it is also leaves young women like Shannon emotionally isolated.

Interestingly, most of the girls at El Valle who adopted this approach were white. During the course of my study, white inmates at El Valle were in the minority (about 10 percent), while Latinas were in the majority (90 percent). Although racial politics did come up in my research, it was not pronounced in this facility compared to larger, adult prisons. Despite this, my research indicated that the girls more likely to fight are Latina. Given the small number of white girls at the facility, they might have been reluctant to fight for fear of retaliation from the Latinas in the unit.

Protective Custody and Perennial Danger

For girls who absolutely refuse to engage in fighting, there is an option of last resort: protective custody. In protective custody, which staff refer to as "PC," young people are housed in isolation and are prohibited from interacting with other young people. They also spend most of their time locked in their cells or exercising alone. Girls who ask for institutional protective custody face constant interpersonal and institutional danger. Other youth in the facility label these girls "PC," which they take to mean "pussy control." Feliz says, "[If you enter protective custody] you're gonna be treated like shit, and no one talks to you. They put the girl I rushed in a separate cell. She is PC'ed, and being a PC is the worst name you can have." Being "a PC" produces the opposite effect of being a shot caller. Instead of respect, girls in PC earn scorn from inmates and staff alike. Correctional officers resent girls in PC because they require more work. Not only do they require close supervision, but also staff must ensure that they do not try to commit suicide and must protect them from attacks by other girls (girls in protective custody are often targeted).

Denise is a seventeen-year-old Latina. She is quiet and serious and has spent a significant portion of her life bouncing between El Valle and local group homes. I immediately notice the multiple tattoos on her wrist and neck, which contrast with her light brown complexion. During an interview, she described how girls in El Valle view individuals who enter protective custody. Denise discussed the consequences of asking for protective custody: "If you PC yourself, . . . you know damn well that they're gonna rush you if you come out [of your cell]. 'Cause that means that either you're a rat or you just don't want to come out of your room 'cause you're scared. . . .

If you come out everybody will jump you, everybody will start bombing [hitting] on you and stuff because you're scared, or because . . . you're a rat." Entering protective custody has serious consequences for girls' standard of living at El Valle. A girl who enters into protective custody is required to be in her cell almost exclusively. Some girls eventually decide to leave protective custody precisely because of the monotony of being inside for extended periods. Once they leave, however, they become the target of physical and psychological punishment from inmates and staff. Protective custody signals both weakness and a willingness to work within the system, two characteristics not much valued at El Valle. Entering protective custody offers temporary relief from assault, but it does not ensure a girl's ultimate well-being.

In this setting, the stigma of being in protective custody is all encompassing. Although girls who directly enter into PC status suffer the brunt of this stigma, youth who associate with them suffer the consequences of this reputation as well. Karen, too, illustrated how this process works: "So, that's how it was like: if you talk to a PC, you're a PC. So the friends of all the PCs, they would get smashed on [beat up], too. . . . I think one PC, and there was four girls hanging out with her, and all of them got smashed on. . . . And I told [the PC], . . . 'Sooner or later they're gonna fuck you and her up. . . . If you keep on hanging out with them, they're gonna do it. . . . They're gonna rock you hard.'" Despite Karen's warning, the girls in this group were eventually assaulted for violating this "rule" at the facility.

The decision to enter PC status is complicated. Why choose self-segregation? At El Valle, PC is often a last resort for ensuring personal safety. Sandy, a Latina in her midforties, is a seasoned teaching aid. Sandy spoke with me about Patty, a student who had been antagonizing everyone. Patty has mild cerebral palsy, and Sandy believed that Patty would probably get beaten up if she ended up in a fight. At the moment when Sandy and I spoke, Patty had several friends who would protect her, which allowed her to antagonize others without much fear. Sandy worried about what would happen when Patty's friends left. She thought most likely Patty would self-segregate so none of the other girls would be able to attack her. Patty had made several enemies, so it appeared that protective custody might be her only option after her allies left. Sandy's prediction was correct: Patty did ultimately decide to PC herself, and she remained in protective custody until the end of her sentence. If she returns to El Valle, she may become the target of attacks once again unless she has friends around who can protect her.

Choosing to Curtail Violence

While correctional staff can promote violence, they can also help curtail it. For example, when Feliz met with her community probation officer inside El Valle, the officer said, "I know you're crazy and you're sneaky, so don't try anything." Feliz continued: "After she said that, I felt I had to act that way because that's what she thinks about me. So I was going to fight. . . . She's only heard of what I can do, might as well show her." Feliz was extremely upset after this meeting. She felt disrespected by these comments, and she wanted to show the officer her "crazy" fighting abilities. As she prepared herself to fight, a correctional guard pulled Feliz aside. Feliz said, "I was gonna fight her then; it was the perfect opportunity to wow my P.O. That's what I was thinking. But then one of CSOs was like, 'Feliz. I know what you want do. It's not worth it. Your mom deserves to be with you [on her birthday].'" Feliz was taken aback by this intervention. In contrast to the staff members who encourage or reward the girls' violent behavior, this particular correctional officer successfully convinced Feliz not to fight. In this case, we can see how institutional actors can both encourage violence and diffuse situations. They clearly influence the girls' behavior.

CHAPTER 3

Legacy Community School and the New Face of Alternative Education

It is an unusually cloudy day in Southern California. I drive the forty or so miles it takes to get to my field site. Over the span of time spent on my fieldwork, I have become accustomed to the glistening blue Pacific Ocean and the bright yellow sun overheard. Now, I seldom notice the natural beauty of this part of the state. I eventually exit the freeway; the ocean is gone. Although the neighborhood I enter has a dingy, worn-down look that reminds me of where I grew up, other aspects are less familiar. I pass by several fields of strawberries, lettuce, cucumbers, and other assorted vegetables before entering the grounds of a small, functioning regional airport. Rusty abandoned airplanes litter an open field, making odd neighbors for the three schools and several other law enforcement agencies located here. The school I am here to visit is housed in a rectangular, peach-colored building covered in decorative stucco and roofed with anachronistic Spanish shingles. With a video camera trained on the main entrance, the building looks more like a storage facility or army barrack than a school. An eight-foot gate surrounds the building, preventing uninvited guests from entering the school and students from exiting without consent. A sign above the entryway reads, "Legacy Community School."

Around 8 A.M., several large yellow buses pull up to the front of the building and drop off students. The young people line up at the door and wait to be searched. They widen their legs and extend their arms in the air. A security guard then runs his hands down each student's legs and arms, patting lightly as he makes his way down their limbs. The students then pass through a metal detector and go on to the actual campus. Most of these students have brown faces and dark hair. The boys dress in baggy black or khaki jeans. The girls wear tight-fitting blue pants and big black hooded sweatshirts, often as a way to conceal tattoos or more revealing outfits.

Just inside the campus, a small courtyard holds six blue tables fixed with adjoining benches. The students often have lunch here during the day. The classrooms and the school office surround the courtyard. As I enter, I see a seventeen-year-old girl with a light brown complexion, wavy brown hair, and a small build. She is wearing dark blue jeans and a white halter top. She seems to be arguing with a teaching assistant; I walk over to get a closer look. As I approach, I recognize the student as Bonita from El Valle Juvenile Detention Facility, whom I introduced in the previous chapters. Bonita first entered El Valle and Legacy when she was fourteen. She, like several of the girls in my study, began having problems at home when she started dating (in her case, dating another girl). Her father, for the most part, is out of the picture, going into and out of prison regularly.

Bonita walks into the class before I can say hello, and I briskly follow behind her and poke my head inside the room. Besides Bonita, I see a twenty-seven-year-old teacher, white, in front of a whiteboard attempting to quiet three Latino students who are talking among themselves. As this takes place, I ask the teaching assistant, who is trying to get Bonita's attention, if I can speak with her; I was hoping to avoid entering the class and thereby disturbing the students. The teaching assistant brings out Bonita, who greets me loudly: "What's up Jerry! Where you been? It's drama at this school, and my teacher hates me." She continues: "I don't like Legacy because . . . I'm practically busted [incarcerated] right here! All of us have been busted before, and you are sending us to the same school where we all know each other? And we are all getting high on the bus. That's why I don't like Legacy." Not only had most of the other students at Legacy also been incarcerated, in other words, but also they had been incarcerated together. This, combined with the constant surveillance at Legacy, meant that Bonita saw little difference between this campus and secure detention.

This chapter specifically looks at how the phenomenon of wraparound incarceration works outside of formal institutions of confinement—in this case, a community day school. I use Legacy's Recuperation Program as a case study to show how wraparound incarceration works. Although in recent years a number of scholars have written on the increasingly common trend of surveillance in schools (Winn, 2011; Bracy, 2010; Price, 2009; Hirschfield, 2009; McGrew, 2008), wraparound incarceration operates in several ways that are distinct from this contemporary practice. In addition to the metal detectors, surveillance cameras, and security officers now common in urban schools, wraparound incarceration extends to include a more constant police presence, at-will drug testing, and official reports from adults affiliated with the associated detention facility. The multidimensional surveillance of girls' behavior is an omnipresent phenomenon, exposing them to both academic and criminal sanctions at school, on the bus, and in the community. The various punishments are doled out by school and criminal justice agents for actual or perceived infractions, or "inappropriate" behavior, in these varied settings. Because of the connection between Legacy and El Valle, the young women I studied were in constant danger of ending up back behind bars for academic or criminal infractions.

Given these circumstances, the young women in my study developed a set of responses, like "going on the run," or avoiding school altogether, to negotiate these constraints. Ultimately, the hypersurveillance that young women experience in the Recuperation Program pushes them to make choices that complicate their lives, often leading them back into the criminal justice system. The relationship between these two institutions and the experiences of the girls in my study demonstrate how they are caught up in the criminal justice system. The three institutions discussed here—the detention center, juvenile probation, and community schooling—are explicitly designed to help and rehabilitate youth. These programs, however, fall short of this goal.

CALIFORNIA JUVENILE PROBATION

According to the California Legislative Analyst's Office (2007), the juvenile justice system is intended to rehabilitate youthful offenders. The adult system, in contrast, is intended to punish. The state uses incarceration and probation supervision as its two central tools in achieving these goals. After minors are arrested, law enforcement agents take them to local juvenile detention centers, which are in turn controlled by county probation departments. According to the state's website, the county probation department can choose to incarcerate these juveniles or to allow local police to decide how to handle these cases. Youth assigned to secure detention by the probation department may be placed, upon their release, on formal probation, on informal probation, on house arrest, in group housing, or in some combination of these.[1]

Currently, county probation departments like the one that operates El Valle supervise 97 percent of all juveniles in the California criminal justice system. This includes young people detained in county detention centers, on house arrest, or on formal probation. Most of the young people at Legacy, and all of the students in the Recuperation Program, are on formal probation. California uses Youth Authority detention centers to house the other 3 percent of youth in the criminal justice system—those who commit more serious crimes or do poorly in local detention centers. These Youth Authority centers are directly controlled by the state. To give a sense of the number of young people under discussion, 222,512 underage individuals were arrested in California in 2005. After arrest, 87 percent of these young people were referred to local probation departments.[2] It is unclear if all youth referred to county facilities eventually ended up on formal probation. Given that young people are typically not held for the entirety of their sentences, it is safe to assume that the vast majority of them eventually ended up on probation.

Once youth are on formal probation, they must fulfill a laundry list of demands to avoid a return trip to secure detention. For example, they are required to meet with their probation officer regularly. During these visits, they are usually drug tested; positive results mean a trip back to detention. Youth on probation are also required to keep a passing grade point average, avoid excessive school absences, and keep to a curfew established by their probation officer. Some youth on probation are also prohibited from spending time in certain parts of the city or with certain individuals. Still other youth on probation are prevented from interacting with gangs or wearing clothing associated with gangs. These so-called gang restrictions are typically doled out to Latino and Latina youth. Finally, youth are restricted from committing new crimes or having any further contact with criminal justice agents. Engaging in any restricted behavior is considered a probation violation, which means that the youth is rearrested and taken to El Valle Juvenile Detention Facility by the assigned probation officer.

In the United States as a whole, a sizeable number of individuals are under formal community supervision. For example, in *The New Jim Crow*, Alexander (2010) argues that over 5.1 million people in the United States are on some kind of probation or parole supervision. She also finds that individuals on probation and parole can be stopped, searched, and drug tested, without their consent, by any law enforcement agent at any time (Alexander, 2010). Several scholars have also found that most people on formal supervision are often rearrested, but usually for violating probation rather than for committing new crimes (Alexander, 2010; Chesney-Lind and Shelden, 2014). This is precisely the kind of danger that plagues the students at community day schools like Legacy.

LEGACY'S RECUPERATION PROGRAM

The inception of Legacy's Recuperation Program—the most direct tie between Legacy and El Valle—is somewhat mysterious. According to interviews I conducted with teachers and administrators, the Recuperation Program began as an idea from a county judge in California's Central Valley. According to respondents, this judge grew tired of seeing the same school-age youth in his court for drug- and alcohol-related violations. The Recuperation Program was therefore designed to provide students with drug and alcohol support, on top of academic support, all funded by a local probation department. It is unclear, however, if the judge intended for the program to resemble anything like its current form. Nor could I find any official record of this judge or his intentions. When the probation department at El Valle first started, Legacy was the only school that agreed to house such a program, which came with extra financial support.

The Recuperation Class operates on a daily and academic schedule that differs from the schedule followed by the larger community school. At Legacy, students follow a traditional "bell schedule," with four to five subjects a day and a break for lunch. The students in the Recuperation Program, however, begin class at 9:15 A.M., and their day is separated into three daily core classes. The instructor provides direct instruction in math and English each day. The third core course varies between physical education, science, history, and independent studies. The students also have time in which to work independently, using a course recovery computer program that allows them to make up previous classes they might have failed. Students who are close to completing their high school credits might also work independently during the entire day while the teacher provides instruction to the rest of the class, sometimes with the support of classroom aides. The structure of the class can vary widely on any given day. For the most part, however, the students leave at 2:25 P.M., except for one day a week when they have a minimum day and leave around noon.

The Recuperation Class is intended to help young people break cycles of substance abuse and negative behavior. The program offers multiple services that provide instruction in education, life, and vocational skills. By far the most emphasis is placed on drug and alcohol counseling. Recuperation students spend about half their day doing academics, and the other half is spent meeting with counselors or probation officers. Usually, half the class goes to a drug education treatment session, while the other half stays in the classroom for independent study or for a core class. Once the first group comes back, they switch. During the transition between the two groups, students are also given a small break. The probation department advertises this drug- and alcohol-education class as a multiagency collaborative program targeting juveniles with severe alcohol and substance abuse issues in addition to a negative school history.

The students in the Recuperation Program receive instruction for every subject from one teacher. Ms. Powell, primary instructor for the Recuperation Class at Legacy, tries to help students earn credits. Her kind and compassionate approach to teaching has helped some of the young people here do well enough to graduate from high school. However, Ms. Powell, like the other instructors at Legacy, is teaching young people who struggle with poverty, multiple forms of discrimination, and the constant presence of the criminal justice system, not to mention drug and alcohol addiction. The Recuperation Class also has upward of half of all students in the general Legacy population with learning disabilities. This means that Ms. Powell must additionally individualize class materials for a large portion of her students, making an already challenging task even more difficult. While youth in the Recuperation Program are able to earn credits at higher rates than other youth at Legacy, many of them still struggle academically.

In the Recuperation Program, almost all of the students have been incarcerated (almost all at El Valle) and kicked out of other schools in the district. Participation in the program requires a referral from a probation officer, so even those students who have not been formally incarcerated have had some interaction with the criminal justice system. The probation department makes these referrals based on an internal assessment process. All youth in this class, in other words, are on formal probation. For them, this is truly the last option.

The Recuperation Program's classroom resembles almost any other classroom at Legacy. The room is about twenty feet long by fifteen feet wide. The walls are white, and the tiles on the floor are white with sprinkles of blue paint across them. The room has two doors, one of which leads to the parking lot and the other to a courtyard. The windows on either side of the doors are reinforced with wire mesh. The front wall holds two bookshelves, a bulletin board, and a whiteboard. Next to the bulletin board is a Smart Board, which allows the instructor to access the Internet and other multimedia tools. To the right of the Smart Board is a teacher's desk, which has a DVD player, a laptop, and assorted stacks of papers. The room also has four computer terminals whose screens are protected by a layer of glass shielding, and which allow some students to work independently. Various posters with basic algebra formulas or images of tectonic plates decorate the back wall. Everything about the classroom seems pretty typical, except for the small office in the back corner with one-way security windows. This office belongs to the classroom's probation officer, who is permanently stationed inside the class.

If the classroom at first glance appears to be typical, the students are not. Aside from the students' specific academic problems, their experiences both in and out of formal detention tend to create certain behavioral issues. First, girls in the Recuperation Program are forced to negotiate constant sexual harassment by the boys in the class. For the most part, boys outnumber girls in this program. Given this uneven ratio, the few girls in the class are regular targets for sexual harassment. Despite signs in the classrooms and around the school that read "Sexual harassment will not be tolerated," sexual harassment is ubiquitous.[3] Drug use, too, is a major problem. Ms. Powell notes that staying sober is the most challenging factor for these students: "For these kids, asking them to stay sober is taking away their whole lives. All they do, all their friends are about, is smoking meth. And all those kids are concentrated here." Most of the students I spoke with had substance abuse issues, the reason for their original entry into El Valle and frequently the cause of their rearrest.

Unlike other Legacy courses, the Recuperation Program works on a "phase" system. This nine-month system has three separate phases. When students complete one three-month phase, they move on to the next. Once students complete the three phases, they can then graduate from the recuperation course and either move into the general Legacy population or, if their school district agrees to it, return to a traditional school. Depending on several other external factors, like paying restitution, some students are also allowed to complete their formal probation once they finish the Recuperation Program. Recuperation graduations, unlike other graduations, take place at the local courthouse, where students are supposed to be released from formal supervision. In practice, however, students seldom complete the program in nine months. For every mistake students make inside or outside of school, such as excessive tardiness, missing class, perceived negative behavior, having a "bad" attitude, or actual criminal behavior inside the classroom, they regularly receive another three months in recuperation—a probation violation—and they are not allowed to "phase up." This means that students can spend an indefinite amount of time in the Recuperation Program.

The Recuperation Classroom and Omnipresent Surveillance

Surveillance at Legacy is constant and ubiquitous, but this is especially the case for youth in the Recuperation Program. Youth in the Recuperation Class struggle with this continual surveillance. For the most part, young people on probation are required to visit their probation officers on a regular basis, but few see them daily. In contrast, students in recuperation see a probation officer every day they attend school, five days a week. As a result, the class probation officer can question students about their behavior at any time.

When an officer named Spencer quizzed Patty, a sixteen-year-old, light-skinned African American who dyed her hair blonde and earned the nickname "Barbie," the intensity of scrutiny became clear. Spencer, a white man in his midthirties who probably stands about six feet and weighs about 240 pounds, asked Patty about a camping trip she had supposedly taken. She replied that she did not go. When Officer Spencer then asked what she did over the weekend, she said, "Nothing." Spencer told her that Patty's mom had called him and had said that Patty missed class on Friday because she went camping. Spencer continued: "She also said it was okay with me [Spencer]; but it wasn't okay with me. I'm on to you." The insertion of a probation officer directly into the classroom gives criminal justice authorities an unprecedented level of access into the details of students' lives, all but eliminating any notion of privacy.

The probation agent in this program also uses students' everyday questions about school or their probation status as an opportunity to engage in surveillance activities. For example, Leticia, a sixteen-year-old, undocumented Latina with a dark complexion, asked Spencer about attending a county fair. He replied, "Why wouldn't you be able to go? That is fine, but go Saturday so you can visit with me." During this exchange, Officer Spencer gathered information about Leticia's weekend plans. While the probation officer might have made plans earlier to attend the fair, now he will most certainly do so. His presence at this nonschool event will mean Leticia and any of her classmates who attend will be subject to surveillance, searches, drug tests, and potential criminal and educational sanctions that they might not otherwise have to face.

Officer Spencer's presence in the classroom was largely negative. While probation officers and law enforcement agents can positively influence students, this probation officer did not. For example, he periodically made disparaging remarks, along the lines of: "Hey, stop being a dumb ass and get to work. Don't use your calculator, use your head." He handled issues related to probation in a similar fashion. One day, for instance, he came into class just as seventeen-year-old Kevin was telling some of the students how "amazing" and "important" he is outside of school. Officer Spencer intervened, saying, "I am the important one." Kevin replied, "You just want to feel important." Spencer said, "I am important. Especially on your court date;

then I am important. You are always like," and he continued in a whiney voice: "Please help me out. I am sorry. I will do good." These unprofessional and disparaging remarks reflect Officer Spencer's general approach to his job in the Recuperation Class. Seventeen-year-old Cathy, whom I first met at El Valle, complained, "He's a dick. He tries to trick you, and he asks, 'When is the last time you smoked?' and then he locks you up if you admit to doing anything. Even if you are doing good, he tries to find something to lock you up." Cathy's statements embody the general sentiments of the other students toward Officer Spencer. Being under surveillance is already challenging, but in this particular case the students also need to negotiate a daily relationship with a less-than-amicable probation officer.

Ms. Powell, too, suffers from Officer Spencer's presence. She said, "He is always trying to sabotage me. He waits [until] a couple of days before we are going to do an activity, and then he makes something up to his supervisor so we can't go. The other PO we had was really good, but this one seems more about punishing them." I experienced this firsthand when I planned a field trip to a local university. While I was planning the event, Officer Spencer remarked, "Why are we taking them to this university? Most of these kids can never get into a school like that. It's stupid." This statement reflected his general outlook, bad attitude, and approach to working with youth in this program.

Testing at Will

Drug testing students at will is perhaps the defining characteristic of wraparound incarceration in the Recuperation Class. Unlike other young people in continuation schools in general, and Legacy in particular, students in the Recuperation Class may be tested for drugs at any time. The topic of drug testing, which was typically referred to simply as "testing," was ever present in the Recuperation Program. It was the constant topic of discussion among students, teachers, and law enforcement agents. This type of surveillance had a host of negative consequences and potentially long-term repercussions for the students.

Drug testing, like the presence of law enforcement agents, was inextricably integrated into the Recuperation Program. Officer Spencer and the other officers pulled students out of class for testing at random. I witnessed several instances when an officer approached one or more students, regardless of whether the students were in class or on a break, to request a test. The only time testing didn't seem random was when someone was due to appear in court. In those cases, testing was almost guaranteed.

For young people on probation, drug testing is nothing new. Most young people on probation are ordered to stay sober; if they cannot achieve this, they face being charged with a probation violation and more time in secure detention. However, most probation drug tests are administered in probation offices or during random visits to the person's home. In recuperation, students can be drug tested at will, and officers can retrieve the results of these tests within a few minutes. Practically speaking, this means students in the class have an increased likelihood of being caught using drugs or drinking.

Drug tests in the Recuperation Program have very real criminal consequences for youth in this setting. On several occasions, students who tested positive for drugs or alcohol were taken directly from Legacy to El Valle. In one instance, Ms. Powell let me know that it would be a small class that day because "Mary, Joseph, Jenny, and Marcus all tested dirty [positive] last week and were taken to the juvenile facility." On a separate occasion, I asked a teaching assistant about Bonita and Cathy only to hear: "They got caught with weed. They are back in El Valle." It was very common to arrive at Legacy, ask for a student, and be told, "Oh, she got locked up."

I spoke to Mary, a nineteen-year-old who was one of the few Native American students in my study. Interestingly, young adults in this county who reach eighteen are often still housed in juvenile detention centers if they have not completed their juvenile probation term by their birthdays. Legal adults, in other words, can still be housed in juvenile detention, though it varies by individual case. Mary was placed in Legacy by correctional officials after serving a few months in El Valle for a nonviolent drug offense. She spoke about testing positive and how she felt about the experience:

> MARY: It bothered me 'cause I got arrested at school, and he [the probation officer], . . . instead of walking me around to the office, he walked me in front. . . . He showed everybody that I got in trouble. . . . I was embarrassed like everybody. It was right in the middle of lunch. He

coulda waited—he coulda done it in the morning and tested me, but he waited until everyone was outside and tested me. Like, "Why couldn't you just wait, or why couldn't you call me into the office and done it there?" He was like, "Oh, I wanted you to feel like whatever for doing that."

JERRY: Is that what he said?

MARY: Yeah, he said, "I wanted you to feel guilty about doing that so everybody could see what you did."

Mary gives us an inside look into drug testing in the Recuperation Program, including how institutional actors can exploit this kind of surveillance. This degrading experience was designed to make her "feel guilty" about testing positive. It also sent a message to other students about the repercussions of testing "dirty" at this school. She mentioned that she was not bothered by being arrested or taken to the detention center. For her, being paraded in front of other people was the most severe and humiliating part of the whole experience. However, these punitive actions did not serve as a deterrent, since they did not prevent her from smoking marijuana upon her release.

It is no surprise that young people in the Recuperation Program, and in Legacy generally, often test positive for drugs. De Velasco and colleagues (2008) found that rates of alcohol and other substance abuse are two times higher for students in alternative schools compared to those in traditional high school. Despite these facts, law enforcement agents continue to use sobriety as a measure of success and a prerequisite for finishing formal probation. However, these practices ignore the personal, psychological, and institutional factors that contribute to these behaviors.

Testing positive for drugs affected students' educational pathways. Students' educational experience and their ability to return to their traditional schools were directly connected to the results of their drug tests. While students earned more time in detention for testing positive, they also earned more time in the Recuperation Program. Moreover, this unique blend of the criminal justice and educational systems means that young people are doubly punished: once by ending up in detention, and a second time by being required to attend the Recuperation Program for extended periods. In other words, students are receiving academic punishment for criminal offenses. This means that young people find it harder and harder to return to their traditional schools and avoid the added challenges they face inside Legacy. Students in the Recuperation Program seldom complete the program, and those who do often take more than the prescribed nine months.

Drug testing and testing dirty regularly prevented youth from leaving the program. Yvette is a second-generation Latina. During a conversation with me, she voiced her frustration with the Recuperation Program: "I have been in phase three for a year. You mess up, and they keep you here. It's like a game. You mess up and have to start over. It sucks. I have been trying to phase out for a year, but I tested dirty." Her periodic positive tests, as well as the institutional response to this behavior, meant that she would spend more time in the Recuperation Class. Young people like Yvette can spend their entire high school career unsuccessfully attempting to finish the Recuperation Program. Anita had a similar experience: "I almost graduated a few months ago. But I tested dirty even though I was clean." For Anita, testing dirty had three key repercussions. She had to stay in recuperation; she could not complete formal probation; and she could not finish her senior year in her home school. While she believed she was drug free, her probation officer said otherwise.

Drug testing at will, especially in the Recuperation Program, highlights one of the key characteristics of wraparound incarceration. Regardless of students' behavior at home or their academic performance, drug testing and the constant surveillance young people encounter in this setting regularly result in the criminalization of their behavior. Smoking marijuana, drinking, or using other drugs is prohibited on every school campus. However, young people at traditional schools do not receive the same criminal sanctions, nor are they subjected to the same constant drug testing, that students at Legacy experience. For example, students at traditional schools can smoke marijuana, drink, and experiment with drugs at home, then attend school the next day. They are not required to be tested in class, nor will they be questioned by a probation officer about their behavior. The youth in the Recuperation Program, like other young people, experiment with drugs and alcohol. The ubiquitous surveillance and punitive sanctions that girls experienced in the program, however, meant that they were often caught up in the system and, as a result, they continually rotated between Legacy Community School and El Valle Juvenile Detention Facility. Young women's experiences in the Recuperation Program are one example of the multidimensional criminalization process that constitutes wraparound incarceration. Anita and Yvette's experiences demonstrate the vicious cycle of punishment that students in the program negotiate regularly.

Trouble in the Community and More Time in Recuperation

Students also earned additional time in the Recuperation Class for infractions they committed in the community. Young people on formal probation might be cited for a probation violation for having contact with the police, testing positive for a controlled substance, or being caught committing a crime. This could result in an informal scolding from a probation officer, time in secure detention, electronic monitoring, or a combination of all three. Like those on probation, students in recuperation are also subject to being cited for infractions that happen outside the context of the classroom. However, they also earn more time in the Recuperation Program for these same probation violations. As noted earlier, students in this program earn academic sanctions for criminal behavior, in this case for behavior that takes place outside of school and away from campus. This practice is unique to Legacy and other community day schools in California and is key to understanding wraparound incarceration. The young women in my study were regularly punished by school and probation officials for behavior that took place in their communities and far from school.

One day I was in the courtyard with several students when I noticed that Jenny seemed unusually detached. She stood by herself and avoided eye contact with me and the other students. I walked over to her and asked how she was doing. She said, "Okay. I got a violation this weekend and I have to start my phase again. I am in the third phase. I would have finished here in January, but not anymore." I asked what violation she was cited for, and she said it was because she had a pipe. She said, "I was walking on the tracks and a police officer stopped me and started interrogating me, and that is how I got violated." Her probation status allowed the law enforcement agent to search her without probable cause, which is how he found the marijuana pipe. Jenny's experience illustrates how students enrolled in the recuperation course at Legacy are punished by having to do more time in the class for infractions that happen in the community.

When young people on probation come in contact with law enforcement agents, they are required to inform their probation officer. If they do not and the probation officer finds out anyway, they can be cited for a probation violation and assigned the multiple punishments associated with this breach. The county probation department and the officers at Legacy receive an electronic notification when people in their caseload experience "police contact." Jenny confirmed this when she said, "One time I got pulled over and nothing happened, but my PO found out anyway. And he tried to take me to court for it. I don't know how, but they find out here." Since Jenny didn't report the incident, she was cited for a probation violation once she returned to Legacy. On top of her displeased probation officer, she had to deal with the looming threat of incarceration. She received another three months in the Recuperation Program. The coming together of the educational and criminal justice systems has created a dynamic juncture between these two institutions.

Youth in the Recuperation Program are doubly punished with criminal and academic sanctions for minor offenses. These offenses can include running away from home, petty theft, truancy, and curfew violations. Allison, a sixteen-year-old Latina, shared her experience of how she earned more time in recuperation. During a visit to a local department store, Allison placed a decorative flower in her hair. She continued shopping and forgot about the flower. She walked out of the store, and a security guard detained her and called the police. She was cited for shoplifting, arrested, and taken to El Valle. When she returned to Legacy, she informed me that she was supposed to complete the Recuperation Program the week she was arrested. Because of this new infraction, she had to postpone her graduation and stay in the Recuperation Program for at least three more months.

Jenny, too, continued to experience trouble at home. After a recent argument with her parents, she ran away but was caught by the police shortly after and was taken to El Valle. Jenny's decision to leave home had several adverse effects. In addition to being placed under house arrest, she was required to spend another three months in the Recuperation Program. Running away was considered another probation violation, and she was kicked out of her medical assistant training program, which was preparing her for an entry-level job in the medical field. This punitive approach to Jenny's infraction does not take into account the factors that contributed to her behavior—in this case, why she ran away from home. Girls like Jenny often run away to avoid multiple forms of abuse (Chesney-Lind, 2010; Chesney-Lind and Shelden, 2014; Schaffner, 1998). The overall experience contributed to Jenny's general feeling that she was in a "rut," especially since she enjoyed the job training and had otherwise been doing well in recuperation. She had been in the Recuperation Program over two years and was only sixty-five credits away from graduating. Jenny wanted to leave the Recuperation Class and enter the larger Legacy School, but her new violation meant that this was not possible. Jenny now felt that her efforts were pointless since she was ordered to spend another three months in the Recuperation Program.

We can see from these examples how the hypersurveillance of young people in the community negatively influences their academic and professional pathways. As I previously discussed, the Recuperation Program is intended to provide opportunities for young people to be successful in school. Ideally this space should provide a unique opportunity for justice-involved youth to become productive members of their community, become sober, and stay away from the criminal justice system. Instead, the constant surveillance and punishment make it nearly impossible to take advantage of these new opportunities. These findings also reveal some of the shortcomings of wraparound services at Legacy. As prior research indicates, the increased contact with the criminal justice system exposes young people like those in my study to more situations where their behavior can be criminalized, instead of putting them on a path outside of the criminal justice system. Wraparound services also prevent young people from eventually reentering the mainstream educational pipeline.

SHOULD I STAY OR SHOULD I GO?

Students in the Recuperation Program develop a set of responses to the numerous constraints of wraparound incarceration. For example, many of the students in the Recuperation Program constantly drink water in hopes of flushing out of their systems any drugs they might have ingested. Other students cope by not coming to school at all. This approach, however, all but guarantees their future imprisonment. In other cases, the challenging conditions that exist under wraparound services encourage young people to make choices that will eventually complicate their lives. For a number of students, the choice comes down to: test dirty and get arrested, or go "on the run."

Going on the run is one way in which students choose to evade and resist authorities, to avoid the punishment of law enforcement agencies and subsequent incarceration (Goffman, 2009). Some girls who choose to go on the run stay away for several months at a time. Alexis described how she decided to run:

> We were blazin' it [smoking marijuana], and I took the best hit ever, and then I turn around and Mr. Paul [the principal] is right there. I had the smoke in my mouth, and I was like, "Fuck." And then . . . I quickly gave . . . the piece [pipe] and the lighter to my friend and then I look at Mr. Paul, who was just standing there, and that's when he said, "I think these girls are smoking dope." Then I couldn't hold it in any longer, and then I just started coughing and a bunch of smoke came out, and I was like, "Oh my God." I had just walked away. I was like, "Okay, I'm not a part of this. Maybe you didn't see me." And then he took my homegirls. And they were walking, and then one of them still had my piece and my lighter and she's like, "Here, Alexis," right in front of his face. So then he brought me along, and then I was like, "I'm gonna book it [run away] right now, guys. I can't get locked up." I always think I'm gonna come back in here for some reason, and I don't want to. So then I was like, "I'm gonna book it right now. Anybody down?" And then Linda's like, "I'll book it with you. I'll book it with you." We ran, and we were under this tunnel for like five hours.

Instead of being caught and sent to El Valle, Alexis ran and hid under a freeway underpass for five hours. Then she proceeded to go on the run for several months. She knew she could not return to her group home or school because of her decision, since she would be immediately arrested at either of these institutions. Instead, she chose to negotiate the dangers of being on the run. Being on the run can be arduous, especially for young women, since they have to constantly negotiate the threat of physical and sexual violence. For many of the young women in my study, these challenges eventually became too much, and they turned themselves in instead of enduring the multiple challenges of being on the street.

Martha, a seventeen-year-old, third-generation Latina, faced a similar dilemma. We were in the school's larger courtyard, where students can play volleyball or listen to music using headphones. A Latina probation officer walked into the courtyard and approached Martha. The officer was dressed in black army fatigues and wore a utility belt that holds pepper spray, hand-cuffs, and other tools. Her dark glasses obscured her eyes. She asked Martha if she was ready to test. Martha replied, "I can't. I just went." The probation officer looked at her and asked, "When can you go?" Martha replied, "I am not sure. I just went," and the officer walked away and said nothing. I notice Martha was wearing dark blue jeans, a low-cut halter top, and a black sweater shirt that she wore only around her neck and chest, leaving her arms and most of her torso exposed. I wondered why she would wear a sweater in eighty-degree weather. When the officer left, Martha walked up to me and said, "Fuck. I'm going to get locked up. I smoked weed and did some coke yesterday. I smoked hella shit, too [meth]. I'm a get busted. I'm fucked! What should I do, Jerry?"

Her question put me, as a researcher and a person who cares for the well-being of these young people, in a difficult position. My suggestions or insights, either way, could have potentially negative consequences. I paused and thought about the options she had available to her. As I cautiously opened my mouth to speak, I heard my voice crack and I cleared my throat. I said, "Well, you can tell her, you can test, or you can leave, I guess." She gave me the same worried look and replied, "Should I go on the run?" I said, "You can leave, but I think it is a bad idea. You are in the middle of nowhere and there is nowhere to go. You will probably get caught." Martha looked down at her shoes and said, "I'm so fucked. And I just got this stupid tattoo on my chest. I was drunk when I got it and it looks stupid. I can't wear any shirts anymore. I want to have it removed. I'm a get in trouble for that. What should I do, Jerry?" Martha lifted her sweater to show me the undecipherable cursive writing on the middle of her chest. She told me the phrase spelled out the name of a local gang associated with her community. She also told me that she has a gang restriction that forbids her from associating with gangs or wearing gang paraphernalia. Her new tattoo would no doubt be identified as another probation violation. Her eyes began to fill with tears as she stared at the floor. She said, "Thanks for listening. I am going to walk for a while," and she began walking around the courtyard, joining several students who did the same.

Martha was able to delay her drug test, but it was inevitable that she would have to test soon, and, given the drugs she took over the weekend, the test would likely be positive. She was left with a serious dilemma: Do I leave and face several days, weeks, or months on the run, or do I test and go back to El Valle? Martha, unlike Alexis, decided to stay and face the consequences of testing positive. Her decision was neither easy nor simple, resulting in a tremendous amount of psychological and emotional stress. For the young people at Legacy, and especially for those enrolled in the Recuperation Program, the threat of incarceration is constant.

RIDING THE BUS: THE CHALLENGES OF
INTERPERSONAL VIOLENCE

Students in the recovery program experience no break from wraparound incarceration. The girls in my study had to negotiate surveillance and violence in school, in the community, and in the places in between. What happens on school buses provides an example of how this process works as girls travel to and from Legacy. For example, riding the bus to school subjected the girls in this study to a whole range of issues, particularly gendered forms of violence. Legacy is in a fairly remote location, making it difficult for most students to get there by walking or by mass transit. As a result, most of the students arrive by bus. There are no surveillance cameras or law enforcement agents on the bus. Bus drivers, however, report any behaviors that they feel violate school policy or criminal law. Given this, girls riding the bus are subject to both criminal and academic sanctions for any infractions they commit there. The girls who ride the bus are often victims of sexual harassment. The close proximity of students while riding the bus also exposes young women to violence and increases the likelihood they will engage in violent behavior. This, along with the regular drug use that occurs on the way to school, often led to additional punitive sanctions for the young people in my study. The bus drivers report criminal violations but do not offer the young people any kind of institutional protection.

A few weeks into the Recuperation Program, Martha began dating one of her male classmates. While the relationship started out well, the boy was often absent from class and she lost interest. Then Eric, another boy from class, tried to kiss Martha on the bus one day after school. When she attempted to reject his advances quietly, he did not desist. She yelled at him in front of everyone riding the bus, and as a result, some of the other students began calling him a "molester." Infuriated, Eric began spreading rumors the next day at school, claiming that Martha had participated in sexual acts with him on the bus. The rumors spread quickly, and Martha began to receive an onslaught of unwanted sexualized comments and behaviors. Her new boyfriend heard these allegations and stopped speaking to Martha. Martha told me that "some of the guys in the program were talking shit," and she felt like she needed to fight them to stop this unwanted attention. Aware of the consequences of fighting at school, she wanted to "try to handle" this problem away from school to avoid picking up another probation violation and a new criminal charge. Like the other components of wraparound incarceration, Martha's story shows how the disproportionate focus on punishment, instead of protection, presents challenges to Legacy students. It also demonstrates the lack of confidence young people have in police and probation officers, given that she elected to handle her problems on her own instead of asking for help from adults in the Recuperation Program.

Bonita, who earlier described Legacy as "just like being locked up," also experienced trouble on the bus, which led to punitive sanctions by educational and criminal justice staff. She told me she "hated" taking the bus because "it was drama." Since youth are bused in from different communities, every neighborhood has a specific bus, and students are supposed to ride only the bus that corresponds to their neighborhood. Often students from different areas would jump on different buses to start fights. The bus was also a place where youth smoked, distributed controlled substances, and engaged in sexual contact. She discussed this experience from inside El Valle after her recent arrest:

> They said they caught me on the bus blazing it [smoking marijuana], and I didn't blaze it. Yolanda tried sitting next to me, and I was like, "Oh, hell no, why you sitting next to me?" So I got up and moved seats, and I was like, "What the fuck! Why are you even blazing it?" I was getting pissed off because she [the bus driver] was blaming me, and she didn't catch me or nothing. And then I was just like, out loud, "I don't give a fuck! I'm still gonna blaze it on the bus." And then what do you know, they call me

out of class. . . . I read the report, and it said, "Ms. Bonita was blazing on the bus, and she even admitted that 'I don't give a fuck, I'm still going to blaze it on the bus.'" So they didn't ask me; they just said that I admitted it. . . . When I got suspended, . . . they said I that I can't ride [the bus] no more because I was blazing it. [When I tried to get on,] they're like, "Get off the bus." I was like, "I'm not getting off the bus. I'm gonna get in trouble with my PO."

While she did not actually smoke on the bus, Bonita responded in a way that incriminated her in front of the bus driver and the other students. Later that day, the principal suspended Bonita and banned her from the bus altogether. She accepted the punishment and stayed home during her suspension. Given the distance between her home and Legacy, Bonita had no other way to get to school. Eventually, she stopped attending altogether, which meant that she picked up another criminal charge.

Riding the bus can also expose young people to interpersonal violence. For example, the bus can become a "staging area" where "campaigns for respect are most often waged" (Anderson, 1999, 77). The bus was a common staging area for students from Legacy, who often fought and participated in other high-risk behavior. Alexis provides an example of the behavior that takes place on students' trips to and from school. A seasoned fighter who had spent some time in El Valle, Alexis was at Legacy when another girl began to give her "dirty" looks and was "talking shit." The girl was trying to coax Alexis into a fight. While Alexis seldom shied away from a fight, in this case she did. She had recently entered a new group home and was attempting to make a fresh start. This new start included staying sober, avoiding fights, and staying out of El Valle. However, she was challenged to fight by this fellow student on the bus. Alexis recounts,

She got on my bus, and she got off in my city, and I was like, "Damn." I told her, "I can't fight you. I'm in a group home; I have too many things on my shoulder right now." And she's like, "Your fear [is stopping you from fighting]." And then I was like, "God, whatever, man, [I'm going to fight] just to shut her up. 'Cause I know she's gonna bug me at school, so just to shut her up I was like, "Okay, whatever." So I got off the bus and we fought. She kind of knows how to fight, but I still kind of beat her up. But we got into it, and then we left. And someone called the cops, and I got in trouble for it.

While Alexis attempted to talk it out, the other girl persisted. Despite Alexis's attempts to diffuse the situation, she decided to fight "to shut her up." While this fight could have occurred without the bus, the mode of transportation facilitated the fight in three ways. First, it brought together girls from different areas and potentially rival neighborhoods. Second, it allowed the girl who fought Alexis to get a ride to her city, something that would have been extremely difficult without the Legacy bus. Third, it provided a location for the fight away from Legacy, where the altercation would have been broken up immediately. While this fight took place away from campus, the bus still exists inside the system of surveillance that defines wraparound incarceration. What happened in this staging area led to punitive consequences for the girls in my study.

As in other settings where Legacy students spend time, getting in trouble while at school, at home, or on the bus can lead to much more serious punishment. At nineteen years of age, Allison is no longer considered a minor. In an attempt to provide her with wraparound services, school administrators allowed her to stay at Legacy while she finished her juvenile probation term and attempted to graduate from high school. One day, while on a school bus headed toward her home city, she began to fight with a fellow Legacy student who was "talking shit" about her. The bus driver called the police, and both girls were arrested. Allison was charged with a felony assault on a minor. As a result, she was expelled from Legacy. Since she is over the age of eighteen, the state does not obligate Legacy to provide her services. The other girl, just sixteen, ended up back in El Valle. Allison was taken directly to county jail and eventually entered the adult state prison system.

BENEFITS OF THE RECUPERATION PROGRAM

Despite the very real challenges Legacy's Recuperation Program poses to girls' ability to escape the correctional system, it did produce some success stories. During the period of my research, approximately five students graduated from the Recuperation Class. These were students who would likely not have graduated from a traditional high school. The larger Legacy School also attempted to work with students who had aged out of the system or had special circumstances. For example, they allowed Jenny to stay and finish earning her last remaining credits at the school, even though she had already completed the Recuperation Program and had aged out of the system. This graduation was doubly significant. Graduation provided Jenny with the necessary credentials for an entry-level position or entrance into a community college. More importantly, students like Jenny who were able to pay restitution and finish the program completed formal probation. This meant they were "free free," or unconditionally unrestrained by the criminal justice system. This is significant, because it means that status offenses (activities or behaviors that are classified as "criminal" by law enforcement agencies only when someone is underage) and misdemeanors will not result in another stint in El Valle. This small group of young people became unconditionally free for the first time in several years.

Other students didn't manage to graduate but nevertheless attained credits at an accelerated rate. For students who had been years behind in their studies, their time at Legacy presented an opportunity to make up lost ground. For many of these young people, this was one of few positive experiences they had with public education. Students benefited from the smaller class sizes and a low student-to-teacher ratio. Ironically, some students, like Bonita, felt more comfortable in this school than in their traditional schools. Several students noted that returning to a traditional school after Legacy felt "overwhelming" or like "too much." Other students told me that they felt Legacy was "more kick back," and that it tolerated more misbehavior by the students. Most young people also enjoyed the increased counseling they received there. In addition, many benefited from job training programs. For some, the increased security felt like structure.

Though initially beneficial, this same structure complicated the lives of students at Legacy and in the Recuperation Program (California Department of Education, 2012c). Despite the modest benefits of the program, most of the students I spoke with preferred to attend their home schools if given the option. But returning to a traditional school would come with its own set of challenges.

CHAPTER 4

School, Institutionalization, and Exclusionary Punishment

I walk into a room and take a seat next to fifteen-year-old Sandra. She greets me enthusiastically, waving her hands and smiling. She and I sit and talk in one of the two classrooms in the girls' unit inside El Valle Juvenile Detention Facility. The classroom is about fifteen feet wide by forty feet long. The cinder-block walls and florescent light fixtures on the ceiling give the class a cold and sterile feel. A large whiteboard at the front of the room features multiple posters pasted to its surface with the phrase "academics, character, and transition." Another poster reads, "Off-Limit Topics: Sex, drugs, gangs, fights, violence, weapons, crimes, staff, body parts, and other inappropriate things." My nose picks up a light, musty odor, common to detention centers, a sign that this is not a traditional classroom. Unlike ordinary classrooms, this one also includes a six-feet-long by four-foot-wide windowpane that provides a view into the day room. You can also see young people's cells, a small exercise yard, and a television bolted to the adjacent wall. As the students sit and receive instruction, correctional staff walk by and peer into this educational space.

Sandra and I chat before class starts. She had attempted to return to a traditional high school after a lengthy incarceration term, but the transition was not successful. I ask Sandra, "Did you go to school on the outs?" She replies, "Nope. I got enrolled, but I never went. I went on the run three days later. I was actually nervous, I didn't want to go to normal school; I wanted to go to continuation school. 'Cause I'm not good with crowds. . . . I have anxiety, like I just can't do it; it's weird. . . . I go to school, I'm smart enough to, but it's just like a mental block that's stopping [me]." Sandra's poignant comment addresses some of the real challenges typical among young people who are returning to a traditional school after having spent an extended time in detention or at a community day school. For Sandra, the large student body and endless possibilities of a traditional school signaled the potential for danger and victimization. While most young women in my study dreamed of returning to their home school, it was often an overwhelming and negative experience.

My study demonstrates how the treatment girls received at their "regular" schools put them in situations that landed them back in detention. The challenges of attending school were exacerbated by the lack of positive support that the girls received from wraparound services once they left Legacy Community School. In fact, the little wraparound support they did receive, like probation supervision and electronic monitoring, actually made them targets for mistreatment at the hands of their peers and educational staff alike. Along with this, the girls were also stigmatized because of the time they spent at Legacy Community School and in El Valle Juvenile Detention Facility. In Sandra's case, those challenges proved too great, and she eventually ended up back in El Valle.

Sandra's story, like those of other girls told here, demonstrates that wraparound services failed to prepare her for a return to traditional school. Instead, these services made her time in traditional school more challenging. As they did at home, in detention, and at Legacy, the girls in my study continued to experience interpersonal violence at the hands of their peers, and they received little protection from school or criminal justice officials. Instead, they experienced institutional harassment and targeting shaped by administrators' gendered and racialized perceptions of these young Latinas as gang members and criminals.

This treatment was exacerbated by the girls' status as justice-involved Latinas. Schools officials often assumed these girls were involved in gang activity because of their previous incarceration, speech patterns, makeup, clothing style, or general attitude. While some of these stereotypes are commonly applied to Latinas and Latinos in American schools (Vigil, 2008; Rios, 2006; Katz, 1997), the justice-involved girls were additionally stigmatized by their time behind bars (Cole and Heilig, 2006; Casella, 2003). Once school officials identified the girls as justice-involved, they were labeled as "at-risk" or "problem" students. These institutional labels led school personnel to target the young women for mistreatment and exclusionary discipline. In most cases, school administrators or police suspended the students or expelled them from school altogether, but no one ever addressed the trauma or challenges of being institutionalized and the unexpected consequences of wraparound services. Nor did these young women receive support from a social worker, educational expert, or therapist for their transition from community day school to traditional school. Once suspended or expelled, youth were rearrested, taken to secure detention, and returned to Legacy.

A number of scholars have identified how young men experience negative institutional labeling through their involvement with the criminal justice system (Rios, 2011; Sharma, 2010; Casella, 2003). However, scholars are still building their understanding of the challenges young women (especially Latinas) face when transitioning from the criminal justice system to traditional school. I focused particularly on this understudied group to provide scholars further insight into the shortcomings of wraparound services. While intended to help, these services make returning to school increasingly difficult for young women like Sandra.

"GOING TO SCHOOL IS TOO MUCH": SCHOOL AFTER INCARCERATION AND LEGACY COMMUNITY SCHOOL

The young people in my study found it extremely difficult to make the transition from the detention center, where every action is planned and regimented by correctional staff, to a large school environment with less structure and what seemed like the potential for constant danger. This institutionalization was a major theme in my research. Institutionalization is "the process by which inmates are shaped and transformed by the institutional environments in which they live" (Haney, 2001). Institutionalization shapes the norms, habits, thinking, and general behavior of previously incarcerated individuals once they are released into the community. (Gover, 2004; Haney, 2001; Goffman, 1961; Skyes, 1958). These behaviors may be apparent immediately after an inmate's release or may emerge once an individual has been out of detention for an extended period. Sandra spoke to this during an interview:

> JERRY: Tell me about going to school.
>
> SANDRA: Well, I usually run away really soon, . . . And over there at school it's harder, 'cause . . . we've been like, girls in here have been insti, instit—I can't even say it.
>
> JERRY: Institutionalized?
>
> SANDRA: Yes! That one! [Laughs.] And then we're used to small, small classes; and we go there, we're in a normal high school, [and] some of us are with a bunch of people, . . . [and] we're not used to it. . . . Some of us freak out. I know I did. . . . My mind and my body still thought I was in here [detention]. So when people walk around me, I have to turn to make sure they're not gonna try to jump me. Or someone was sitting in my seat, and I was like, "Well, are you trying to punk me or what? Get up." . . . So I think she was trying to make me look stupid. In actuality, she was just sitting in a chair.

Sandra keenly describes the lingering consequences of her institutionalization. The classes in detention are much smaller compared to classrooms in traditional schools; for her, smaller classes mean fewer people to potentially fight in a dangerous situation. She also identifies the anxiety that she experiences in this setting. The defensive behaviors that she developed at Legacy became overwhelming in a setting that has a perpetual ebb and flow of people. Small behaviors like a "dirty" look, an accidental bump, a disagreement in class, or someone sitting in "your" lunch seat can create a tremendous amounts of stress. This stress and anxiety contributed to girls' violent displays in this setting. These sorts of behaviors, which derive from institutionalization, are challenging to identify, treat, or negotiate, since they often emerge unexpectedly and without warning (Gover, 2004; Haney, 2001; Culbertson, 1975; Goffman, 1961; Skyes, 1958). Some girls avoid school altogether, citing these overwhelming feelings of discomfort as a reason for not attending. Sandra's comment illustrates that girls' reentry from previous incarceration can have very real physical, psychological, and institutional consequences.

Most of the young women in my study spoke about "awkward" or "uncomfortable" feelings among the large groups of students who attend traditional schools. Research on incarceration and institutionalization finds a similar dynamic. In a review of empirical work on this subject, Haney (2001) found that "institutionalization . . . renders some people so dependent on external constraints that they gradually lose the capacity to rely on internal organization and self-imposed personal limits to guide their actions and restrain their conduct." This dynamic is even more harmful among young people, since they are more susceptible to the effects of institutionalization than adults who end up behind bars (Gover, 2004; Haney, 2001; Culbertson, 1975; Goffman, 1961; Skyes, 1958). This anxiety often left the girls in my study feeling irritable. Others identified overwhelming feelings of vulnerability. Given these feelings, the young women in my study often moved quickly to address perceived threats or disrespect by fighting. Girls like Sandra would get into "too many" fights when returning to a traditional school setting. In these young women, the lack of structure in traditional school, compared to El Valle and Legacy Community School, induced these unwanted reactions.

Traditional Schooling and Problems in Class

Girls who returned to traditional school also struggled with teachers' pedagogical approaches. A majority of the girls I spoke with complained that teachers in traditional school did not care about them. They felt teachers didn't want to teach them, or they observed that the teachers didn't take the time to answer their questions. Girls also mentioned that teachers told them they needed to "pay attention" or accused them of being "lazy." The girls felt school was "boring" and not relevant to their lives. Instructors demonstrated this by not answering students' questions, by ignoring them, or by asking them to leave class altogether.

Fifteen-year-old Melissa shared these same feelings about teachers' lack of interest in her educational outcomes. She juxtaposed her experiences in public school with those at a small independent study program:

> It's different because [of] the way they teach us at [independent study], and the way they teach us in . . . [public school]. . . . Here [at independent study] they actually try to get to know you. . . . They don't [in public school]. . . . [They] just judge you by how you appear, so they might not like you 'cause you don't pay attention. But in [independent study] they just try to get to

know you and stuff, and they make you feel much better. I feel much better letting my teacher know how I feel and letting her know about me. 'Cause I feel like I'm her friend.

In the independent study program, Melissa believed, teachers were genuinely invested in her educational and emotional well-being. She therefore made an attempt to attend regularly and tried to do well academically. In public school, she felt teachers judged her by her appearance and baggy clothes, which teachers often associate with gang-affiliated Latina and Latino youth. For example, in her study of Latino students in San Francisco, Katz (1997) found that teachers often associate Latino and Latina heritage with being an active gang member, whatever a student's intellectual capabilities. Other research has found that regardless of students' actual behavior, school officials often treat Black and Latino students like criminals (Vigil, 2008; Rios, 2006; Cammarota, 2004; Katz, 1997). As Katz put it: "The process of criminalization may begin with false perceptions, but deepens when any possibility for success is blocked within the mainstream" (1997, 80). In my study, I found that the false perceptions of students as criminal gang members had a highly negative effect on youth. These young people also believed their teachers did not want them in class because of their status as probationers and the stigmatization as justice-associated youth.

The youth in my study complained about more than stigmatization; they identified specific pedagogical issues that made their transition to a traditional curriculum more difficult. Mari, for example, was one of the few students to successfully complete the recuperation program at Legacy Community School. When she returned to her home school, however, fifteen-year-old Mari had trouble with her teacher's pedagogical style, "Well, she was nice, but . . . she would get me frustrated. . . . I would ask her to help me, [and] she wouldn't help me. . . . She said that I had to pay attention; but I was paying attention. . . . It would get me mad." Several students made similar complaints, saying that their requests for explanations were answered by admonitions to "pay attention." Mari believed herself to be completely dedicated to her academic studies, and she felt her teachers treated her with hostility no matter what she did. Her sense of alienation is not uncommon for Latina and Latino students, who often feel they are not wanted in class or that they are being treated with disdain (Vigil, 2008; Rios, 2006; Camma-rota, 2004; Katz, 1997), a dynamic that is compounded when teachers believe Latinas and Latinos are affiliated with gangs or the criminal justice system (Romero, 2001).

Despite her efforts in class, Mari could not grasp the academic material. Receiving no help from her instructor, she eventually gave up and ultimately stopped attending school. Mari's trouble in class could be attributed to a lack of academic continuity or to an undiagnosed learning disability. Whatever the real source of her difficulty, her schoolteachers attributed her failure to a lack of dedication to her studies or pointed to her experiences in the criminal justice system as evidence that she could not be successful. Interactions like this often left youth feeling angry and alienated. When girls like Mari did not get the help they needed, they often acted out in class, which in turn got them in trouble at school. According to my participants, this lack of class-room support was detrimental to their academic development and often resulted in their return to El Valle, Legacy, or both.

These experiences were consistent across a range of academic skills. The young people in my study experienced this treatment regardless of their academic or intellectual gifts. For example, Luna is a nineteen-year-old Native American woman who has lived her whole life near the city of El Valle, where El Valle Juvenile Detention Facility is located. She had a similar experience while attending a large public high school. Despite hav-ing attention deficit disorder, Luna excelled in academics in the detention center after being kicked out of her home school. Eventually she earned her GED by working independently behind bars. This was an impressive achieve-ment, given that she attended formal high school for approximately one year only. But with her learning disability, she struggled in traditional classrooms:

[School work] makes sense to me, but I have to read it a couple times, . . . especially math and English. [I can] follow it, [but] it takes a little longer. But that's why they didn't wanna put me in slower classes [special education classes]: 'cause I would pass all my tests but just not respond in class. That's why they'd get mad. That's why they kicked me out: 'cause I just don't pay attention. . . . So it's like they never took the time to talk to me about it; they just thought I was a bad kid who didn't wanna go to school.

As happens to many students with learning disabilities, Luna's classroom behavior and perceived lack of concentration resulted in her receiving negative attention from school personnel. This negative attention was also connected to her teachers' perceptions of her as a "bad" kid who would ultimately leave school and reenter secure detention. In her study of teenage violence prevention, Prothrow-Stith found that "[teachers'] confusing of behavior and attitude with intellectual ability go[es] along with a general trend among teachers to view street-wise adolescents in a negative light" (1991, 166). In this case and in other research, teachers often associated Latina and Latino students' perceived or actual negative behavior with a lack of self-control or associated it with subpar intellectual abilities (Rios, 2006; Cammarota, 2004; Katz, 1997). Educators' inflexible teaching approach, negative view of Latinas, and rigid expectations for classroom behavior were not congruent with the educational needs of the girls in my research. These problems were significant enough that a large portion of the girls in my study gave up on school altogether.

The young women in my study also noted that traditional schools were insensitive to the challenges specific to previously incarcerated girls. For example, girls felt these schools did not offer sufficient therapeutic services, nor did their schools acknowledge the hurdles posed by stigma. Alexis experienced this firsthand after she was released from El Valle Juvenile Detention Facility. She, like many of the youth in my study, was placed on house arrest, which meant that she was required to wear an electronic ankle bracelet. Like her peers, Alexis attempted to hide her anklet with baggy jeans or sweatpants, but she ran into trouble with the dress code. In Alexis's case, the problem came during her physical education class. Her teacher instructed her to wear shorts and gave her no other option. She tried to explain, but her teacher still required her to wear shorts. She said, "I went into the locker room, and I came out with P.E. shorts. . . . I had long socks, and I tried pulling them up all the way; but you could still see the thing, and people were trippin' out. . . . And I remember some girl's like, 'Are you on house arrest?'" Other students began to question Alexis about house arrest, detention, and her criminal affiliation.

This regular harassment agitated Alexis and made her already challenging time at school more difficult:

As soon as you walk into the door, people start judging you. . . . I was at [gym], and this little mob of girls . . . dawged me out [gave me dirty looks]. . . . And [one of them] even turned, and I was like, "What the fuck are you looking at?" And then she's like, "What the fuck?" And then I was like, "What, you wanna get down with me or something?" . . . And then her and her friends started getting crazy. I was like, "Oh my God. I'm gonna get jumped right now."

Alexis describes returning to public school as being "too much drama," where she encountered constant waves of peer harassment, specifically peer harassment tied to her status as a justice-involved youth and a perceived gang member. While this harassment might seem innocuous, it had extremely negative consequences for the girls in my study, girls who are accustomed to handling threats of interpersonal violence with a stern physical display.

The stigma of being incarcerated has very real educational and interpersonal consequences for these young people. School policies like the dress code did not help the girls navigate the transition, and eventually most of them experienced embarrassing and traumatic events like the one Alexis describes. In order to avoid this stigma, some young people left school for extended periods. Some stopped attending school altogether, which often led to their being cited for a probation violation, eventual arrest, and more time in secure detention or at Legacy Community School.

Interpersonal Violence and Traditional School

As happened elsewhere in their lives, the girls in my study had to deal with interpersonal forms of violence at a traditional school. Most of the girls I spoke with attempted to stay away from fighting. However, their reputations, the stigma of being incarcerated, or their perceived gang affiliations often led to physical fights with students at school. Denise experienced this when attempting to return to her home school after successfully leaving Legacy Community School. After she was released from detention, she was placed in a group home by local authorities who decided her mother could not provide a stable living environment for her and her siblings. At school, students began to question her about her involvement in the criminal justice system and her connection to a local gang. Since she was from a neighboring city, most students in this new school assumed she was a part of a rival gang. She said during an interview:

[At school] everybody started calling me "shithead," just 'cause I'm from [El Valle] and not here [this city]. They thought I was from the gang, . . . [and] everyone started disrespecting, calling me names. . . . I didn't say nothing during school, but once school was out . . . I could not take it no more. My anger just busted out [and I got in a fight]. . . . I don't like to go through all that process, people asking me, "Oh, where you from," or "Oh, my God, I can't believe you're in placement," or "Oh, my God, I can't believe you were locked up."

Denise describes the taunting and teasing she experienced at her new public school. Students constantly asked her about being incarcerated or in a place-ment home. According to Denise, this teasing and bullying often occurred without school administrators intervening on her behalf or providing her with a viable option for avoiding this behavior. Having reached a breaking point, she responded the same way she would in detention: she engaged in a physical fight. She eventually ran onto a crowded bus and fought several stu-dents simultaneously. Her probation status made her vulnerable to serious sanctions, and she was expelled from her new school, arrested, incarcer-ated, and eventually returned to Legacy Community School. Her anger and frustration were compounded by the fact that she has experienced this treatment at every traditional school she has attended. Given this, she even-tually decided not to return to this school or any other traditional high school, to avoid harassment.

Jackie, a fifteen-year-old Latina, similarly attempted to avoid fighting at school. However, the harassment by other students proved to be over-whelming, and she too decided to fight. Jackie described her experience: "There's a girl; she was picking on me a lot. Like, she would be bumping into me, and she would be saying things to me, and I would ignore it. . . . And after school I'd see her at the park, and that's when I started beating her up. The next day I got arrested at school. I got expelled." Jackie describes how she was kicked out of school and arrested for fighting off campus. Given the mistreatment she was experiencing, she eventually felt she had to "handle business" to make this bully stop. In detention, this approach to dealing with this issue worked (and was encouraged); in school, it proved to be the wrong decision. Like Denise, she was arrested and taken to El Valle for an extended period.

The challenges that I have described thus far are directly connected to the girls' previous time behind bars and involvement with wraparound services. Given that the girls' reenrollment at a traditional school had to be approved by the school district, it was inevitable that school officials, including teachers, administrators, and campus police, learned about the girls' justice-involved status. Among other things, enrollees must present their academic transcripts, which list their time at Plazo Correctional School and Legacy Community School. In a study of two high schools in the mid-Atlantic states, Bracy (2010) found that school officials use this sort of insider information to target students for "focused" attention, which often means exclusionary punishment such as suspension or expulsion. For their part, students learn about girls' time behind bars from seeing girls getting dropped off by a group-home bus, observing probation officers directly speaking to youth, noticing an electronic monitoring bracelet, or through gossip. Others students simply assume the girls are justice-involved because of their dress, mannerisms, or makeup. We can see, then, how the markers of wraparound services expose young women to new and unique challenges without providing additional support.

RACE, GENDER, AND EXCLUSIONARY PUNISHMENT

The challenges described in this chapter, including trouble with reentry, stigma, and fighting on campus, are common to youth who have been previously incarcerated (Winn, 2011; Winn, 2010; Sharma, 2010). However, the girls in my study also needed to negotiate gender harassment and culturally specific institutional harassment when returning to traditional school. According to youth, the teachers and school administrators often targeted them because they perceived them to be gang members and justice-involved youth. While I did not observe this dynamic directly, this was a common theme during my interviews with these young people, and it is likely that girls' behavior was interpreted in the ways I describe in this section.

First, teachers' erroneous perceptions of my research participants as "bad" girls, "gang members," or "criminals" made the girls stand out from other students. School staff compared these previously incarcerated young women with other "good" Latina girls, who were passive and quiet, and who did not challenge their authority, all traits associated with "proper" gender behavior (Garcia, 2012; Dietrich, 1998; Segura, 1993). School officials also believed these previously incarcerated young Latinas were not interested in school, because they wore clothes and makeup that the officials associated with gang affiliation and activity. The criminalization of Latino and Latina youth culture is not new (Rios, 2011; Vigil, 2008), but school officials' perceptions of Latinos and Latinas as cholos and cholas, or gang members, negatively influences youths' experiences in the educational pipeline. School staff's negative gendered and racialized perceptions of these previously incarcerated young women drove staff to look for small and large infractions that would allow them to suspend or expel them. These negative perceptions had very real consequences for girls, since a suspension or expulsion was a probation violation and resulted in another arrest and their eventual return to El Valle.

The girls in my study told me that school administrators had negative perceptions of them on campus. Previous research in this area demonstrates how school employees' negative perceptions of students, especially students of color, can result in real, and often criminal, consequences for students (McGrew, 2008; Casella, 2003). Interestingly, the consequences of this labeling are often more severe than the actions that get students in trouble in the first place (Casella, 2003). Alexis poignantly described how these negative perceptions were directly tied to her race and ethnicity. Unlike most of the other girls in my study, Alexis attended an affluent, predominantly white school after her release from El Valle. She said of her experiences there: "I was in school in this white community. At the time there was only white people, and I was the only Mexican; and I stood out. I hated it. I hated it. . . . Nobody wanted to talk to me. . . . I used to draw on my eyebrows, [and] they were scared of me." As the only Latina on campus, she found that her classmates were afraid of her presence at school and actively avoided her. The other students complained to their parents and teachers that Alexis made them feel unsafe. When the parents learned that Alexis had been spending time with older community members, they complained to school officials. The racialized views of teachers, parents, and students at school made Alexis feel isolated. Eventually she felt she was being targeted for removal by school officials who did not want her on campus. Students began challenging her to fights before, during, and after school. In her account, school officials seldom punished the students who were harassing her. This institutional and interpersonal harassment was directly connected to the staff's and students' racialized and gendered perceptions of her as a gang member who posed a threat to students and the general safety of the school.

The girls in my study mentioned that teachers treated them poorly after they realized the girls had been incarcerated or on probation. School officials on occasion would tell them, "You shouldn't even be here," or would suggest they leave school indefinitely. This hostile treatment took place in as well as out of class. Debby, whom I introduced earlier in the book, described her experiences after getting into a disagreement with one of her teachers: "I got kicked out my second day 'cause my teacher said . . . [after a disagreement], 'Your probation officer will talk to you about this.' . . . And I said, 'You don't even know my probation officer. . . . You best believe I'm gonna call her.'" During this time, Debby was new to this school; she was attempting to acclimate to her surroundings. At that point, she did not realize anyone knew about her formal probation. Debby was infuriated that the teacher would divulge this information in front of the rest of the class, and eventually she left the room.

Rasta, too, believed that she was targeted by school administrators. Unlike the other girls, she is a poor white girl. At her school, she had an extensive negative reputation for being sexually promiscuous and regularly insubordinate. This negative institutional label followed her to all the schools she attended. She described her reputation and how it influenced her academic experiences:

RASTA: Ever since I go to school I've had this reputation that follows me from school to school, and it kinda sucks.

JERRY: What reputation?

RASTA: "Oh, she'll tell you what to do. She'll curse you out. She'll skate away around at school. She gets in fights a lot. She destroys property. She kicks it with a bunch of rough boys." I'm like, "Oh, great." It's not so bad; when I first went to El Valle, and they read my name off the list, they looked at me like I was crazy. They're like, "Oh, so you're Rasta," and I'm like, "Uh huh." They're like, "Oh, I don't see why'd they say those things about you."

Rasta's reputation followed her from school to school. Even before she could establish a new identity, these negative perceptions influenced her time at school. Through her narrative, we can see how powerful institutional labels are, and how young women are punished for violating gender norms. In the eyes of school employees, Rasta violates several key gender expectations. For example, she fights and destroys property, which are not things that "good" or "reputable" girls do (Jones, 2010; Jones, 2008; Collins, 2004). While Rasta did not have to deal with the racialized discrimination the other girls in my study did, she was preemptively targeted and eventually punished for her deviation from gender expectations.

The youth in my research described exclusionary harassment and punishment at the hands of teachers, particularly when teachers meted out classroom discipline. During an interview at the El Valle detention center, seventeen-year-old Annabelle described how teachers treated her at her regular school:

> The teachers hated me. . . . They would be so disrespectful. Like, "Oh, what are you doing here?" Like, you are "worthless," . . . that kind of shit. [They would say,] "You're not even capable of learning this stuff." . . . In science class . . . he [a teacher] would just always snap at me. . . . If I would talk or something, he [the teacher] would put me outside in the hallway, and when other people talked, "Oh, just talk. It's okay." You know? And one time he did that to me, he put me in the hallway, so I just left. . . . And then I got suspended.

From Annabelle's perspective, she received differential treatment in class, treatment that she ascribed to her race and gender. While it's unlikely that teachers actually "hated" these students, girls came to believe that this was the case, which in turn caused them to act out. Current research demonstrates that teachers often view Latina and Latino students with suspicion and contempt in the classroom (Vigil, 2008; Rios, 2006; Katz, 1997). This gendered and racialized treatment was exacerbated by Annabelle's history in the criminal justice system. Eventually, such treatment resulted in more severe discipline for the young people in my study.

The girls in my study identified a specific pattern that resulted in their removal from school. First, teachers identified them as "problem" students. According to girls' accounts of life at school, this dynamic was very common. When returning to traditional school, girls often felt as if they were subject to greater levels of surveillance compared to their peers, usually because of gendered or racialized perceptions of these girls as "loud," "violent," or just bad students (Winn, 2011; Morris, 2007). In other words, girls' behaviors, especially those that challenged normative gender expectations, were often met with sanctions from teachers. School staff then continued this mistreatment or waited for a student to make a mistake that eventually earned her a suspension or expulsion. Other teachers simply harassed students until they stopped attending school altogether. This behavior made the youth in my study feel alienated from their educational experience and hated by teachers in traditional school. Eventually most of these young women stopped attending school.

Removing Students

The girls in my study experienced multiple forms of institutional harassment at the hands of school officials and teachers alike. Amber, whom I first met in secure detention, described how the process of targeting students for removal from school works. She was kicked out of elementary school, middle school, and high school before she began living on the streets. During our conversation, she discussed how school principals "hated me"; they began targeting her for removal from school. Amber said, "They treat me different. [They said,] . . . 'Just don't come, Amber. If you don't like it, just don't come.' . . . And the principal even told me like, 'I don't want you in my school.' . . . And they even kicked me out." Amber recalls how principals at her schools would target her for minor infractions like tardiness, slowly increasing the severity of her academic punishment. Eventually school administrators managed to expel Amber from every level of public education. After her last expulsion, she was arrested and sent back to Legacy Community School, where she stopped attending school entirely. The finding that staff expel youth because of their negative perceptions of them is common both in other research (McGrew, 2008; Casella, 2003) and in my own work.

Feliz, like Amber, recalled that after leaving Legacy and returning to a traditional school, she got along very well with teachers, "but the principal and all that hated me." Although Feliz had a good relationship with her teachers, the school administrators only grudgingly approved of her presence in school, given her reputation as a drug user, her previous involvement with the criminal justice system, and her probation status. Feliz said, "I was treated so differently. . . . I was singled out." She continued:

> One day I was going to class, and there was about twenty other kids running to class 'cause the bell already rang; and I was walking, and a lot of other kids were walking, on their phones and talking and stuff. The principal came up to me, and she's like, "Why are you late?" I was like, "I dunno, I'm sorry, I'm just walking to class." The principal said, "No stay out here." I was like, "Okay." And she called my teacher, and the teacher was fine with it. But the principal was like, "Feliz's late, and she's not even supposed to be here."

After Feliz's return, she became a target for harassment at the hands of school administrators who felt she was "not even supposed to be here." Regardless of the reasons for which Feliz continued to be harassed, she was eventually expelled during a dubious school drug search in which she believed she was the sole target. Feliz, like other youth in my study, felt she had become a target for removal from school because of her race, gender, and previous incarceration.

Karen, a seventeen-year-old white girl, received punishment for trivial offenses at hands of her teachers, just as Annabelle had. During her time at public high school, Karen complained, teachers often "disrespected" her in front of class. Consistent with my other findings, Karen's experiences embody the differential treatment the girls in my study received in class. "[The teacher would say,] 'Oh you guys need to respect me.' . . . And one time I remember I was writing, and she was talking, and I saw her coming toward me. . . . And I look up, and she was gonna snatch my pen, and I was like, 'What are you gonna do?' And she was like, 'Give me your pen.' And she was fighting with me; she could've just told me to stop, you know? . . . And the whole class was looking." Karen said that her teacher regularly took points off her grade for being late, stared at her while the class was working, and scolded her for small infractions. Karen believed these events were directly connected to her experience in secure detention. Like other youth, she often felt teachers singled her out for regular punishment while ignoring the poor behavior of other students. In Karen's eyes, there was no way for her to escape this poor treatment, whatever her behavior or efforts in the academic arena. In this particular incident, the teacher's attempt to take Karen's pen escalated into a larger physical exchange in which Karen and the teacher became the focal point of the class. Karen was eventually expelled for this incident and was returned to Legacy.

CHAPTER 5

Hooks for Change and Snares for Confinement

The stories of girls like Debby, Aracely, and Maria detail their attempts to escape the cycle of wraparound incarceration. Having faced multiple forms of abuse in the home, these girls ran away, only to be arrested and sent to El Valle Juvenile Detention Facility. This was the space in which most of the girls I studied experienced wraparound services for the first time. Their narratives demonstrate how their lives changed once they were in secure detention. The continued surveillance that followed them out of El Valle and into Legacy Community School eventually led to more time behind bars. For those individuals who managed to return to traditional high school, their experiences as justice-involved youth complicated their attempts to return to a normal life. Given these complicated circumstances, it is important to understand whether, and how, girls can successfully transition to adulthood after getting caught up in the criminal justice system.

Feliz, a seventeen-year-old Latina introduced in chapter 1, provided me with the first glimpse of success experienced by young women in my study. While she was a well-established shot caller in the detention facility, she was also a gifted student who managed to graduate high school well before her nonincarcerated peers. Over the course of my fieldwork, I collected data on the few cases of young women who successfully left the criminal justice system. Their experiences contrast with those of young women who wanted to leave criminal pathways but were unable to do so because of their formal probation status, tumultuous home life, or other challenges that characterize justice-involved youth and young women receiving wraparound services. My findings contribute to scholars' understanding of criminal desistance and the gendered nuances of young women's pathways in and out of delinquency.

LIFE COURSE, GENDER, AND CRIMINAL DESISTANCE

Feminist criminologists have long argued that criminal desistance for women is unique and largely connected to positive family ties and a healthy home environment (Carbone-Lopez and Miller, 2012; Pollock, 2002; Belknap, 2001; Owen, 1998). Similarly, life course scholars have long argued that, for men, getting married is key for exiting criminal pathways (Sampson and Laub, 1993; Sampson and Laub, 1992). However, getting married or even establishing a long-term partnership can have the opposite effect for women. Findings from a survey of three hundred men and women in a "shock incarceration" program in the Midwest revealed that, for women more than men, finding a spouse or long-term partner can contribute to future offending (Benda, 2005). Other scholars have also found similar patterns (Alarid, Burton, and Cullen, 2000). This is often the case because women are more likely to engage in drug and criminal behavior when men are involved in their lives than when they are not (Wyse, Harding, and Morenoff, 2014; Carbone-Lopez and Miller, 2012; Capaldi, Kim, and Owen, 2008; Gelsthorpe and Sharpe, 2006; Haynie, Giordano, Manning, and Longmore, 2005; Owen, 2003; Simons et al., 2002). Conversely, forming a family with a caring partner serves as a buffer against future offending for women and as a means for criminal desistance (Benda, 2005). In a survey of five hundred multiethnic women living in a poor urban area of Denver, Colorado, researchers found similar results. Kreager, Matsueda, and Erosheva (2010) found that becoming a mother was strongly associated with a consistent decline in delinquency and a drop in drug use over time. They argue that motherhood, instead of marriage, is a key turning point away from crime. This was especially true for poor women of color living in this urban area. Wyse, Harding, and Morenoff (2014) found that, for previously incarcerated women, having a partner often helped provide economic support, supervision, and a place to stay, which initially helped keep them away from criminal activity. However, these same partners often contributed to drug use, domestic violence, and eventually more criminal involvement (Wyse, Harding and Morenoff, 2014). This double-edged sword was common among women who lacked economic support and a safe home, and who struggled with family issues (more so than men) when attempting to leave criminal pathways (Wyse, Harding, and Morenoff, 2014; Carbone-Lopez and Miller, 2012; Mclvor, Trotter, and Sheehan, 2009; Barry, 2007).

Justice-involved women were able to avoid criminal pathways in three key ways. First, overcoming substance abuse issues was critical. Staying sober was often an uphill battle, since women usually become entangled in this system through drug use and dependency issues (Carbone-Lopez and Miller, 2012; Mclvor, Trotter, and Sheehan, 2009; Hanna-Moffat, 2003). Scholars have also found that developing a sense of personal agency and moving away from the control of others helped women stay out of the criminal justice system (Mclvor, Trotter, and Sheehan, 2009; Hannah-Moffat, 2003). Developing a sense of agency was key, since women and girls are often encouraged or coerced to participate in crime and drug use by the men in their lives (Mclvor, Trotter, and Sheehan, 2009; Díaz-Cotto, 2006; Hanna-Moffat, 2003). Finally, scholars found that when community parole or probation officers help women in transition with housing, drug rehabilitation, and other social services, the women are less likely to reoffend (Mclvor, Trotter, and Sheehan, 2009; Holtfreter, Reisig, and Morash, 2004; Zanis, Mulvaney, and Coviello, 2003). These discussions of criminal desistance are important for understanding how young women leave the criminal justice system.

Scholars have argued that pathways to crime are curtailed when individuals develop strong social bonds within institutions like schools, family, work, or the military (Owen, 2003; Giordano, Cernkovich, and Rudolph, 2002; Sampson and Laub, 1993; Sampson and Laub, 1992; Sampson and Laub, 1990; Elder, 1985). These transitions depend on "turning points," or "hooks," where people can successfully leave deviant pathways (Giordano, Cernkovich, and Rudolph, 2002; Sampson and Laub, 1993; Sampson and Laub, 1992). Building on the life course research related to "hooks for change" and on feminist criminology, I identify the key turning points that led girls in my study from detention to college, gainful employment, or the larger California prison system. I reveal the key moments in the girls' development when they appeared most ready and willing to make a positive change in their lives. My findings shed light on the key factors that educators and criminal justice agencies can look for when attempting to make positive interventions in young people's life trajectories.

To illustrate these broader patterns, I provide three cases of young women who were able to leave the criminal justice system. I also offer three examples of young people who were ready, but unable, to leave the justice system, and who instead entered the adult corrections system. Both the successful and unsuccessful cases give scholars and practitioners insights into how young women change their lives. First, I found that the young people in my study needed to experience a cognitive transformation wherein they viewed criminal justice agents and other practitioners in wraparound services as kind and compassionate allies. This shift is similar to what other scholars have found, but it is unique in that young women do not have to shed their own "deviant" identity to experience positive change. Young people can continue to participate in deviant behavior, and still experience positive change, as long as they are not caught and so long as they view law enforcement agents in a positive light. Second, as other scholars have also found among young women in the criminal justice system, my participants benefited from becoming pregnant. This gender-specific experience gave my participants the motivation to mature and become ready for change; or, alternatively, it served as a catalyst for staying sober. Becoming pregnant also encouraged the girls in my study to finish their formal probation terms. Finally, the young women were inspired when they experienced life as a "normal" person uninvolved with the criminal justice system. These experiences helped them understand what a healthy and productive life is like away from detention and wraparound services. When the youth in my study experienced one or a combination of these transitions, they often decided it was time to leave the criminal justice system. Some girls were so deeply ensnared in this system, however, that their desire to leave was curtailed by wraparound services.

Even with a change in mind-set, the young women in my study could not change their lives without first achieving two key milestones. First, they needed to get off formal probation if they were to exit criminal pathways for a significant amount of time. The requirements of formal probation were by far the most challenging components of wraparound services. After an initial arrest, young women were frequently rearrested for probation violations, commonly known as "bootstrapping," instead of new offenses. Second, the young women needed a stable home in order to complete formal probation. Girls in the foster care system, girls with abusive parents or guardians, or individuals without stable housing seldom completed their probation terms. Young women in my study were also more likely to exit criminal pathways if they stayed sober. Becoming sober was not, however, always a necessary component of leaving this deviant life.

The key finding here is that young women require as little contact as possible with the criminal justice system and wraparound supports if they are to eventually escape this broader system. The more contact these young women have with criminal justice agencies and wraparound services, the more likely they are to get caught up in this system. The young people in my study who did not get off formal probation or could not secure a safe living situation did not leave the criminal justice system, despite experiencing a positive cognitive shift, getting a taste of life away from this institution, or becoming pregnant.

COMPLETING PROBATION AND WRAPAROUND SERVICES

Young women who successfully complete their probation terms are quite likely to exit the criminal justice system. Completing probation can be extremely difficult and was by far the most challenging component of wraparound services. During my research, I documented only four cases of young people who successfully finished probation. But when the young people in my study managed to complete formal supervision, they often stayed out of the criminal justice system for extended periods. Feliz accomplished this by graduating from Plazo Correctional School, which is located inside El Valle Juvenile Detention Facility. During Feliz's six visits to the facility, she accumulated enough credits to graduate high school early. Over the course of my two-year investigation, more than one hundred girls passed through the walls of El Valle, but few graduated while in detention. Graduating high school while in detention can be challenging, since youth are required to negotiate two sets of rules and regulations imposed on them by detention center and education officials.

During her attempt to finish high school in confinement, Feliz experienced multiple institutional challenges. Apart from students' performances in the academic setting, students are graded on a four-point behavior scale. Feliz received one point, the lowest point on the scale. She said, "I was supposed to graduate this Friday from high school, and Ms. Marcy and Ms. Sanchez basically said 'no' because of my behavior. They're dangling my fucking diploma [in front of me] 'cause I got a one instead of a four in here." Feliz discussed how the teachers at Plazo held her back from graduating. Both instructors in the unit told Feliz she could not graduate because she had behaved poorly in class, even though she had the academic credits and met other requirements necessary to complete high school. One of the teachers let me know that jail administrators, too, were not on board with Feliz's graduation, given her recent behavior.

After this initial setback, Feliz improved her behavior, at which point school officials told her she could not graduate because she was missing one and a quarter credits. Feliz told school officials she had taken another course at a separate school. Since school staff could not verify this information, Feliz had to retake this course and further postpone her graduation. These sorts of administrative complications were very common for young people attempting to graduate Plazo, Legacy, or a comprehensive school. Students who attend Plazo often struggle to get the credits they earned at the multiple schools they attended. Similarly, when they leave detention, their new schools do not always receive their transcripts; others refuse to accept the credits. This is especially the case at traditional high schools, where administrators are less likely to accept coursework completed in detention or might refuse students altogether because of prior incarceration.

After approximately ninety days of negotiating with detention and school officials, Feliz earned the one and a quarter physical education credits she needed to graduate. After six stints at El Valle, over 365 days in detention, and multiple enrollments at a local community day school, Feliz graduated. Most importantly, she finished formal probation and would no longer receive wraparound services, meaning no more house arrest, drug testing, probation officers, or attending the Recuperation Program. Feliz achieved what most girls at El Valle never do: unfettered, unrestricted freedom. After leaving El Valle, she enrolled at a local community college, where she is currently pursuing her bachelor's degree.

Probation is a form of institutional labeling, a practice that significantly affects life course development relating to crime and noncrime outcomes (Hagan and Palloni, 1990a). Scholars have argued that life course research needs to "examine social ties to both institutions and other individuals in the life course, and identify their transitions within individual trajectories that relate to changes in informal social control" (Sampson and Laub, 1993, 18). In Feliz's case, a key turning point was getting off formal probation. Feliz and her experiences demonstrate how severing formal ties to the criminal justice system can help young people transition away from criminal pathways. In other words, Feliz was able to leave the criminal justice system by shedding the negative institutional label and the formal wraparound supervision that contributed to the criminalization of her behavior. These findings are consistent with other research on labeling and the criminal justice system (Sampson and Laub, 1993).

Experiencing a Cognitive Shift

Jenny is an eighteen-year-old Latina, introduced earlier in this book. She first entered the El Valle Juvenile Detention Facility when she was twelve years old. She was initially arrested on a possession charge and was referred to a court-ordered drug rehabilitation program designed for young people with substance abuse issues. Over the course of the next three years, she struggled to stay out of detention and was expelled from every school in her district. In the tenth grade, school and detention officials referred her to the Recuperation Program. In this new class, she struggled to stay sober and received more citations for probation violations after testing positive. Jenny also struggled because of her low academic skill set and few high school credits, since she had not attended school regularly. During her time in recuperation, however, she began to adjust to attending school daily, despite being occasionally arrested for probation violations in the community and on campus. Unlike most of the other young people in my study, Jenny eventually finished the Recuperation Program.

Jenny was one of the few students who created a positive relationship with the recuperation classroom's probation officer. Research on life course theory identifies the importance of increased bonding for young people involved in deviant behavior (Sampson and Laub, 1993; Sampson and Laub, 1992; Sampson and Laub, 1990; Elder, 1985). This bonding is especially important in key institutions like school, family, and work (Sampson and Laub, 1993; Sampson and Laub, 1992; Sampson and Laub, 1990; Elder, 1985). Jenny discussed how her perception of her probation officer changed after she spent several months in the Recuperation Program.

> JERRY: What was it like having a PO in a class with you?
>
> JENNY: It was nice, 'cause he would support me a lot. . . . At first I just thought they were out to get me. But then I realized that they were trying to help me.
>
> JERRY: How did you come to that realization?
>
> JENNY: I don't know. It was just how they would talk to me when I was down. . . . [And] when I had this bad boyfriend, and they found out about it, they would come to my house about every week . . . to check up on me.
>
> JERRY: And what did that do?
>
> JENNY: It made me realize that they are just trying to help.

Jenny discussed how her perceptions of the probation officer stationed in the recuperation classroom changed over time. While most of the young people (and the teacher) viewed this law enforcement agent with contempt, Jenny's view of him changed when he began checking in with her at home and when she was struggling in the Recuperation Class. These home visits and conversations at school can be perceived as routine police investigations. Jenny, however, believed this officer's actions demonstrated genuine concern for her safety and well-being. This perception and the subsequent relationship they developed helped Jenny shift her negative view of this agent and the Recuperation Program as a whole. This cognitive transition took place when she began to see the officer as a caring adult, instead of as an institutional actor tasked with punishing her behavior. This transition helped change her long-term path in a deviant life-course trajectory.

Although Jenny's perceptions of the Recuperation Program and the probation agent had changed, she continued to regularly test positive in school. During our interview at Legacy, she excitedly told me she was going to graduate in two months. Shortly after this conversation, she was "busted" (incarcerated) for testing "dirty" (positive) in the Recuperation Class. I had a follow-up conversation with her inside El Valle Juvenile Detention Facility after she was arrested. She shared with me how she was still having problems with her mother at home. To deal with anger and other unresolved issues, she occasionally ran away or smoked marijuana, two choices that resulted in her rearrest when in the community or when she returned to the Recuperation Class. Although it took her longer than two months to graduate, Jenny's new attitude about school sparked a change in her family life as well. Her parents became more supportive as she spent more weekends and evenings at home. She began doing well in school and attempted to stay sober.

After Jenny's perceptions of this program changed, I asked her, "Overall, what were your experiences in recuperation?" She responded, "Recuperation is a challenge." Jenny cited the program rules and the frequent drug tests as the most difficult components of the program. Despite these challenges, she was happy to be in the Recuperation Class, where she was able to work toward her high school diploma. Jenny spent the next twelve months trying to finish two months' worth of classroom work. Eventually, she completed the Recuperation Program and her formal probation term. Once she finished recuperation, Legacy School officials let her stay on campus despite being a legal adult. She then spent another twelve months finishing high school in Legacy's general student population, eventually receiving her diploma. While she was initially scheduled to graduate in 2011, she did not finish her high school career until 2013. In Jenny's case, the nine-month Recuperation Program took thirty-six months to finish.

Once Jenny completed the Recuperation Program and left Legacy, she was off formal probation and no longer received supervision from the juvenile justice system. Jenny attempted to enroll in a local community college, but with budget cuts and overenrollment becoming more common across the state of California, she found it difficult to successfully integrate into college. She eventually found a job at a local department store and managed to stay out of secure detention. The limited income that this job provided, and her inability to gain a college education, however, also curtailed her ability to leave her parents' home and become completely independent.

Finding a Stable Home

Cathy is a seventeen-year-old, third-generation Latina. I first met her at El Valle during a math class. She is an unusually cheerful young woman with a history of serious substance abuse issues. Nine months after I started conducting fieldwork at Legacy Community School, I ran into her in the Recuperation Program. Cathy, like Jenny and Feliz, was one of the few successful cases in my study. Like these other two young women, she managed to finish the Recuperation Program and successfully left a life of using and selling drugs. Unlike the other two cases, however, Cathy became pregnant while in the Recuperation Program and while on formal probation. Getting pregnant was, in her case, a key experience that helped her become sober. Getting sober was also an important factor when completing the Recuperation Program. While her pregnancy helped with this transition, the biggest turning point for Cathy was finding a stable home environment.

Cathy had struggled with a turbulent home environment; she often attributed her substance abuse to her home life. She shared her experiences with me after she was released from El Valle and placed in Legacy Community School by corrections administrators. During a physical education class, Cathy and I sat on the hot concrete floor and talked. She told me she had trouble staying sober and was smoking marijuana, drinking every day, and selling cocaine and methamphetamine to earn money. She recalled that it was easy to stay sober in detention, and said that she was struggling to keep her sobriety now, with "everything else that [was] going on" in her life. As we spoke, her response confirmed scholars' understandings of home instability and how this factor leads young women to the criminal justice system.

As we sat in the P.E. yard, Cathy explained the challenges she had with her stepfather. She said, "When I was younger he put a camera in my room, and there was a hole where he could look into my room." She also believed that, along with this intrusive behavior, her stepfather had molested her when she was a child. Cathy discussed how, apart from this, he would regularly "mess" with her and give her a hard time about trivial issues. Eventually, he removed the door from her room so that she had no privacy at all. She told me that she felt conflicted, because she wanted to do well and go to school, but that she was living in "a place that is not good for me." As do so many young women in her situation, Cathy began dating a much older man—in this case, twelve years her senior. When her parents discovered this new relationship, they called the police. After this, a huge family fight ensued in which she punched her brother and was almost attacked by the family dog. She said, "I tried to leave and take a break; but I could not leave, because I was on house arrest. So I just started going crazy and dropped to the ground and started to cry." After this fight and the end of her house arrest, her mother agreed to let her live with a friend without reporting any of these events to her probation officer.

After moving out and living away from home, she began doing better in class. She established a good relationship with the Recuperation Program's teacher, who was helping her catch up on previous coursework that would eventually help her graduate. Cathy was doing well until Ms. Powell went on maternity leave and was replaced by a substitute teacher. At this point, Cathy decided she no longer wanted to be in the Recuperation Program, because she "didn't like" the new teacher. When Ms. Powell returned, Cathy was able to continue with her academic progress. In the meantime, Cathy continued to struggle with substance abuse and received multiple citations for probation violations and return trips to secure detention.

As I walked into the Recuperation Class during a routine visit, she ran up to me and said, "I might be pregnant. I can't smoke or drink anymore; it makes me sick." Previous scholars have found that becoming a parent is a key factor for leaving criminal pathways (Carbone-Lopez and Miller, 2012; Pollock, 2002; Belknap, 2001; Sampson and Laub, 1993; Owen, 1998). This is especially the case for young women (Kreager, Matsueda, and Erosheva, 2010; Benda, 2005; Giordano, Cernkovich and Rudolph, 2002). Once she became pregnant, Cathy was able to stay sober and avoid El Valle. For Cathy, her pregnancy and her new, stable home became the catalyst for positive change. The support she received from Ms. Powell also helped her focus her attention on academics. After approximately five years in high school and over twelve months in the Recuperation Program, she graduated and enrolled in a local community college. These events ultimately shaped Cathy's pathway away from the criminal justice system. For Cathy, becoming pregnant was the central motivator for becoming sober. However, her positive changes would not have been possible without access to a stable home.

The young women in my study were able to exit criminal pathways in several ways. First, they experienced a positive cognitive shift wherein they believed the Recuperation Program, the probation agent, and wraparound services were genuinely intended to foster their well-being. This was true for Jenny and Cathy, despite the extended time they spent in the Recuperation Program and the multiple probation violations they were cited for while in this class. Cathy's and Jenny's experiences support the findings of prior research on the importance of social bonds to institutions like school. These two cases also demonstrate that law enforcement agents and other people who work with justice-involved youth can be seen as compassionate and can eventually help change the lives of girls.

Second, young people need to have a stable and safe living situation. In the case of young women, I believe the importance of finding a stable home environment has been overlooked; it is especially important given the gender-specific abuse young women experience in unstable homes and the further mistreatment they receive on the streets once they run away (Winn, 2011; Winn, 2010; Chesney-Lind and Shelden, 2014; Simkins et al., 2004; Kakar, Friedemann, and Peck, 2002). This was especially the case for Cathy, who had to regularly negotiate the threat of sexual violence at home.

Cathy also demonstrated how having a child can be a beneficial and gendered pathway for leaving a life of crime. Becoming pregnant gave her the necessary motivation to stay sober and avoid probation violations, accomplishments she could not master before becoming pregnant. Pregnancy is an important event when attempting to leave the criminal justice system. But as I discuss later in the chapter, becoming pregnant without a stable home negatively influences young women.

Feliz's case demonstrates that a young woman can leave the criminal justice system even without staying sober or having a positive cognitive shift, so long as she completes the terms of her probation and finds a stable home. Her case is unique in that she was the only young person in my study able to complete high school and her formal probation while incarcerated. After her release from detention, Feliz was off formal surveillance; she did not need to stay sober or "buy in" to the services and supervision imposed on her by the criminal justice system. For the young women in my study, experiencing a positive cognitive shift was irrelevant if they did not get off probation and did not find a stable home.

During my research I also found that several young people were ready and willing to change, but were unable to do so given their extended formal and informal ties to the criminal justice system.

Snares for Confinement

Ray has been in and out of the criminal justice system since she was twelve years old. As a child, she struggled with poverty and multiple forms of gendered abuse at home and in her community. As a young teenager, she became pregnant and then started doing drugs after she got the "baby blues." Her postpartum depression was exacerbated by her difficult home life and the incarceration of her child's father. During our last interview she recalled, "That's when I started messing up. . . . That's when I started doing drugs." Unlike in the case of Cathy, who used her pregnancy to stay sober, Ray's early introduction to parenthood complicated her life and was one of the leading factors that contributed to her first contact with the criminal justice system. Ray provides one of the most compelling cases of a young woman who wanted to get away from the criminal justice system but could not do so successfully.

Ray, like Feliz, graduated from Plazo Correctional School. Once she was released from El Valle as a nineteen-year-old, she attempted to reintegrate into her community and find gainful employment. At first, she had little success, but eventually she found a part-time job selling knives with a small door-to-door sales company. She quickly realized that traveling with knives was a "bad idea," since she feared she would be tempted to use them in self-defense if she encountered trouble on the street. She then found full-time employment processing strawberries in the large agricultural sector in the area. Ray worked the night shift for approximately a month. Initially, she struggled with the grueling workload and ten-hour shifts. Despite this, she acclimated well to this environment. She began to develop a routine of going to work, spending time with her son, and regularly checking in with her probation officer, all of which kept her from returning to secure detention.

After a month of success, however, Ray was hurt at work. She said, "I was fixing the machine for the packaging . . . and it sliced my finger. . . . And I had to go to . . . the hospital. And then . . . they said, 'We'll call you,' and they never called me back, so . . . I got injured and they laid me off." Although firing an employee because of an injury at work is illegal, Ray had little economic or material recourse with which to fight this decision. Her new injury meant that she found it even harder to find employment. With few marketable skills, she decided to enroll in a local community college.

As a graduate from Plazo Correctional School, Ray felt confident that she would do well in community college. She was also excited about pursuing a career as a social worker. Her probation status required that Ray attend school, work, or participate in a combination of both of these activities, which also motivated her decision to register at community college. When discussing the enrollment process, she said, "I did the registration or whatever, [and] I went to go take the test. . . . But I did badly on the English part and the math part, . . . and I haven't enrolled after that." Ray struggled with the advance placement test required of all newly enrolled students in California community college. She was required to take several remedial math and English courses before beginning the actual college curriculum. Faced with what seemed like an insurmountable amount of coursework, she did not return to college. But since she had not yet found a different job, her decision also meant that she was actively violating her probation. She stopped checking in with her probation officer as well. Shortly afterward, the probation department put out a warrant for her arrest and she was officially "on the run."

Despite her warrant, Ray continued "laying low," alternating between living with her mother and new boyfriend. However, she found it difficult to stay away from the police. She said, "I was just playing around and just started running 'cause I was so bored and I couldn't find no jobs. . . . Then I was visiting my mom, . . . but both [my brother's and uncle's] probation and parole [officers] came while I was visiting. And they ran my name, and— ta-da!" During a visit to her mother's house, Ray was arrested for violating probation. Like many of the young women in my study, Ray had intergenerational links to neighborhood gangs and the criminal justice system. Given this, her mother's house was a routine stop for law enforcement agents. After Ray was arrested, she was taken to adult county jail for the first time. She said, "County is ruthless. At [El Valle] you get some type of advice . . . and resources, you know? And in county you just didn't get anything at all. They just lock you up and leave you there." After a few days in county jail, however, she was sent back to El Valle to serve the incarceration term associated with her juvenile probation. After she completed her time in detention, Ray was released on adult probation, which requires her to meet with a probation officer for the next three years. If she violates adult probation, she will return to the adult county facility or could potentially end up in the state prison system.

Her time in county jail made her reflect on her experiences in the criminal justice system and the very real possibility that she could end up in prison. Ray provided insight into the cognitive transformation process she experienced after her trip to county jail:

> Now I like paying bills. I like my own money that I get on a regular basis. Now I think about: "If I go with this person [to use drugs], I'm going to forget that I have this appointment tomorrow, and then I'm not going to go to work this day." And I just think it's just a pain. I just rather not deal with it. . . . And I woke up one day at two in the morning, and I was like, "I don't want that." . . . It just went through my body, through my mind. . . . I don't know how to explain it, honestly, . . . [but] I'm tired of this.

At nineteen, Ray discussed how she has grown tired of going in and out of the criminal justice system. She has been on some kind of formal supervision for the last seven years, and now she is ready and willing to change. She attributes that desire for change to a combination of her experiences in county jail and a taste of gainful employment.

Giordano, Cernkovich, and Rudolph (2002) identify a readiness to change as key to successfully exiting criminal pathways (see also Boyle, Polinsky, and Hser, 2000). But despite her readiness to change, Ray continued to be involved in the criminal justice system. This took place primarily because of her formal probation status. Once Ray exited El Valle, she faced many of the same circumstances that she had previously struggled with in the community. She struggled with finding employment outside of the low-paying service sector and with integrating into community college with a very low academic skill set. Her material supervision meant that her failure to succeed in either of these areas kept her locked into the criminal justice system, regardless of her desire to stop her criminal behavior.

Experiencing an Alternative to Deviance

After eight months away from El Valle, fifteen-year-old Alexis returned to secure detention five months pregnant. Eight months was the longest time she had been away from the facility since she had first arrived, as a twelve-year-old girl. When we walked into the interview room inside the unit, she said, "Well, all my makeup is gone, and now I'm a little chubbier. . . . I'm carrying a baby." As we sat and talked she discussed what she had experienced after leaving El Valle and how she returned to secure detention. Her narrative illustrates the multiple challenges she encountered in the community and how they eventually resulted in her readiness to leave the criminal justice system.

When Alexis was first released, eight months before our conversation, she attended one of the 283 community day schools in California. At this school, which was similar to Legacy, she experienced similar patterns of constant surveillance. At her new school, she began fighting, and she continued to struggle with substance abuse. Even worse, some of the other girls began challenging her to fight because of her neighborhood affiliation. Given her probation status, Alexis decided she could not fight on campus. Despite her reluctance to fight, the other young women were challenging her on campus, eventually following Alexis onto her bus. She told me, "So I got off the bus, and we fought; and someone called the cops and I got in trouble for it. And then, [some other girl] got arrested, and I was like, 'Oh, they're gonna do that to me.' . . . So I ran away." After the fight, the police arrested a young woman whom they mistook for Alexis. And after Alexis witnessed this arrest she decided to go on the run.

While she was on the run, Alexis's drug addiction became worse. During her time on the streets she stayed in a house with other methamphetamine users and distributers, or she simply wandered the city. She said, "I was using meth heavily. . . . I was staying in the streets. [And] when you are on meth, it's just, you just stay with one person, and the day and night just doesn't matter." The cycle that Alexis describes is very common for young people who leave secure detention. Upon their release they often struggle with the same issues, such as substance abuse and fighting, that got them in trouble with the criminal justice system in the first place (Chesney-Lind and Shelden, 2014). After wandering the streets and using drugs for a few weeks, Alexis met a twenty-one-year-old man who invited her to stay in his home.

Scholars have found that women often begin romantic partnerships when they are attempting to negotiate the dangers of being on the streets (Díaz-Cotto, 2006). Alexis began living with this new man. She said, "I didn't like him at first. . . . I would ditch him in the beginning, and so every chance I got I would take advantage of him." Alexis describes her rationale for dating this man. Initially, she needed a place to stay, and this individual insisted on her being his "girlfriend." She agreed to this new relationship, but she did not take the union seriously. After a few weeks, however, she began to develop feelings for this person, and she embraced the new partnership.

Several months into her new relationship, her partner became "obsessive." First, he encouraged Alexis to stay home and stop using drugs and alcohol. Initially, her boyfriend and his controlling behavior helped her stay sober. She was grateful for his help, but his behavior became even more controlling. He began calling her multiple times a day to see if she was home. He also regularly accused her of being unfaithful with their mutual friends. This behavior began to cause problems between the two, and they started fighting several times a day, which intensified when Alexis found out she was pregnant. She said, "I stressed out a lot, and he didn't understand that, . . . now that I'm pregnant, I would always be crying and stressing out. So then I was like, 'This isn't healthy for the baby.'" After this self-revelation, Alexis decided that, after six months on the run, it was time to "do the right thing" and turn herself in to the authorities to complete her probation. Eventually, she left a note at her boyfriend's house and turned herself in at a nearby police station.

Back at the facility, Alexis explained the two reasons she desired to leave the criminal justice system. The first was directly connected to her pregnancy. I asked, "Does it feel different, now that you're pregnant?" And she replied, "I feel more mature, kinda. I feel like an adult now. Well, 'cause I kinda have to grow up; when I'm raising my kid, I can't be immature about it." Interestingly, this new desire for positive change was also connected to her experience of living with her boyfriend. She said, "I was a good girl; like, I would help clean and cook. I was a normal girl for once. Except for the fact that I had a warrant. I didn't feel judged. I wasn't in a group home and here [El Valle]. Like, 'I can do whatever I want.'" . . . They [the boyfriend and his mother] went out to eat; it was nice. We didn't have to worry about money, and . . . I could eat whatever. So that was kind of nice." As had Ray, Alexis got a taste of life away from the criminal justice system. For the first time in her life, she was able to feel normal. This sense of normalcy came largely from meeting normative expectations about gender and participating in behavior associated with being a "good" girl, instead of that associated with being a young woman involved in the criminal justice system. Previously, the circumstances of her life had been controlled by older family members or by a group home, Legacy Community School, El Valle Juvenile Detention Facility, or some other branch of the criminal justice system. Her new experiences gave her a glimpse into a potential future that was normal and in which she was well adjusted. Experiencing an alternative life away from the criminal justice system was one crucial way the young women in my study became ready for change.

After sixty days in El Valle, Alexis was released. She moved in with her aunt because she believed this would provide a better environment for her future child than moving back in with her partner. When she eventually contacted the baby's father, a full-blown custody battled ensued, making raising a baby and completing probation more challenging.

Despite Alexis's desire to change, she continued struggling: with substance abuse, three years of juvenile probation, and this new custody battle. Her experiences shed light on the rationale young woman use in entering and staying in abusive relationships with older men, and they simultaneously show how becoming pregnant and living as a "good" girl can positively shape young women and their desire for positive change. This desire, however, was not enough, and she continued to have contact with the criminal justice system.

Contact with the Criminal Justice System and Pathways to Prison
Some young women who have turned eighteen by the time they leave El Valle quickly find themselves saddled with adult felony convictions and several years in state prison. Katie, an eighteen-year-old white woman, provides a key example of this process. She, like most of the other girls in the

facility, had become coming into and out of detention from a very early age. Katie also established a reputation for fighting inside the girl's unit. Despite her regular participation in fights, she also excelled in academics. Without attending traditional school, Katie was able to earn almost all of her classroom credits at Plazo Correctional School inside El Valle. Toward the end of one of her detention terms, she had almost completed all the necessary coursework to graduate high school. Corrections administrators therefore decided to let her stay in the facility to help her complete high school.

Katie continued to make progress toward her diploma, but she also continued to fight. During an administrative meeting that I attended, one correctional officer discussed Katie's fighting, saying, "They dropped all the charges for Katie, but they put six years on her max time. If she continues this behavior she will be placed at the California Youth Authority for six years." Katie's most recent fight had earned her the potential to spend more time in secure detention. At most county-controlled detention centers like El Valle, individuals can be held only for one year. This is considered their "max time." At the same time, a person can also earn more "max time" at the facility where she is being held, or on probation, or at a different juvenile or adult detention center in the state. In this case, Katie did not earn more time at El Valle, but she earned the potential to spend six more years in a state-controlled detention center like the California Youth Authority or on probation upon her return to the community.

Eventually, Katie successfully completed her high school diploma. As in the case of other graduations, teachers and correctional officers came to her graduation ceremony, where everyone applauded Katie's efforts and her dedication to finishing her high school career. Graduations are among the few occasions where both sets of staff (educational and correctional) come together to celebrate the success of a young person. The ceremony was even more significant in Katie's case, since young women graduate less often than young men. Despite this positive achievement, Katie had also earned an adult assault-on-a-minor charge for fighting in the unit. Because of this new offense, correctional officials sent Katie to adult county jail and then to California state prison the day after her ceremony.

Katie's experience is typical, since the few successes in the lives of justice-involved youth are often overshadowed by more time behind bars.

What is important to take away from this case is how the well-intended efforts of corrections personnel led to additional incarceration. As discussed chapter 2, fighting in corrections is often a premeditated investment in one's own safety. Once young people become adults, however, they receive more severe punishment for the same behavior that previously protected them. Katie, who was already technically "free," having served out her term, agreed to stay in detention in hopes of completing her high school education. Despite her positive goals and the good intentions of the detention center staff, this decision led her to the larger prison system. The more contact young people have with criminal justice agencies and agents, the more likely their behavior will be criminalized by these institutions. Katie's case and the other successful cases I present in this chapter underscore why it is important for young people to get out from under formal surveillance and stay away from the criminal justice system if they are to leave criminal pathways.

Conclusion

In my research, I initially set out to investigate the experiences of young women attending school behind bars. Once I began fieldwork at El Valle Juvenile Detention Facility, however, I gained a new understanding of education, incarceration, and wraparound services. I quickly discovered the connection between El Valle and Legacy Community School, and my focus shifted. My research reveals a powerful, multi-institution, circular process that leads girls from home to detention to school, to home to detention to school, and so on. Focusing specifically on Latina girls between the ages of twelve and nineteen, I investigated how these young people negotiated the dynamic conjuncture between school and detention. The girls' ability to escape this system was complicated by one probation department's attempt to provide wraparound services, which are more akin to wraparound incarceration. This book sheds light on the unintended consequences of wraparound incarceration and how this well-intentioned service complicates the lives of young Latinas negotiating the American educational and penal systems.

In recent years, scholars of criminology, sociology, and education have paid more attention to the connection between schools and institutions of confinement (Winn, 2011; Winn, 2010; Morris, 2007; Chesney-Lind and Jones, 2010; Chesney-Lind and Shelden, 2004). Research in this area has primarily focused on youths' experiences in schools and increased surveillance in this setting (Winn, 2011; Winn, 2010; Díaz-Cotto, 2006; González-López, 2006; Simkins, Hirsh, Horvart, and Moss, 2004). Less work in this field has investigated how young people's pathways to deviance are shaped by the increasing material and economic ties between schools and the criminal justice system. Even less work addresses the unique experiences of the growing numbers of young Latina women who are navigating these multiple institutions. My work begins to fill the gap in these current studies; I also show how institutions like the home influence my participants' criminal trajectory.

Certain key home factors can destabilize girls' lives and eventually shape their pathways to incarceration. For example, girls experience multiple forms of abuse before entering secure detention, and this physical, sexual, and psychological maltreatment is directly tied to intersections of race, class, gender, and sexuality. After such treatment, my study participants began dating. According to their parents, this new display of independence and sexuality violated traditional views of "proper" and "respectable" femininity and appropriate behavior for young Latinas (Garcia, 2012; Collins, 2004), which led to further abuse of the latter. Eventually the young women in my study grew tired of this treatment and moved in with a partner or friend or simply lived on the streets. The new challenges they experienced there directly resulted in each girl's first arrest and subsequent incarceration in El Valle Juvenile Detention Facility.

Once released from El Valle, the girls were subjected to increased surveillance, whether through probation, electronic monitoring, or supervision in a group home—all part of wraparound services. The girls often violated conditions of formal probation, with the result that they drifted in and out of California institutions of confinement.

While most texts describe the experiences of Latina girls after they are involved in this system (Díaz-Cotto, 2006), few works describe the ways in which the first contact is made. Even less research addresses how girls, and especially Latinas, navigate life after experiencing abuse in the home. This glimpse into the lives of Latinas sheds light on the multiple points of intervention for individuals looking to help at-risk girls before they become involved in the criminal justice system.

The experiences of these young women also demonstrate some of the limitations of wraparound services. These young people already had difficult home lives, and the wraparound services they received after their contact with the criminal justice system further complicated their lives. While wraparound support is intended to provide youth with support at home and school, this is not happening. For example, one of the girls I interviewed, a twelve-year-old, pregnant elementary school student, had received no counseling, social-work support, or other help to deal with her victimization, home abuse, and loss of her child. After being arrested and subsequently placed on probation, however, she regularly had to deal with the criminal sanctions associated with this supervision. Both the stigma of having been previously incarcerated and the problems associated with leaving probation force girls to make difficult choices as they pass into adulthood. If wraparound services are intended to help youth in the community stay out of detention, why are they not designed to help girls like the ones I've discussed deal with their abusive home lives and new drug addictions? Are these services designed only to punish young women?

Wraparound services also did little to help the young women in my study negotiate life inside El Valle Juvenile Detention Facility. Once girls are incarcerated, their lives change. As at home, they encounter the constant threat of danger when in detention. And while researchers have documented the multiple ways that young people first come into contact with the criminal justice system, less work has demonstrated how their lives change once they are behind bars. Current research on crime and criminal desistance also tells scholars little about the new challenges young people face in detention. This is especially the case for young women and girls who are currently incarcerated. Some incarcerated young women strategically resort to violence to keep themselves safe (Flores, 2013), despite the fact that fights come with consequences such as added sentence time, physical harm, or loss of privileges. Those who fight fit into two distinct identities: the shot callers, and those who fight only when necessary. Both recognize the benefits and consequences of choosing violence. For girls who establish themselves as individuals who can behave violently, their behavior means that their cells are less likely to be searched, and that correctional staff members are less likely to disrespect them in front of other inmates. Some girls may defer to these shot callers or seek their guidance. The shot-caller reputation not only keeps the girls safe but also elevates their status among inmates and staff. Girls who refuse to fight unless it is truly necessary also maintain some of these benefits: the key in this presentation of self is the willingness to fight when challenged.

Those who do not fight choose either to isolate themselves or to have the institution isolate them via protective custody. The girls in my study who resorted to relational isolation to keep themselves safe are similar to those in Jones's (2010) study on urban African American girls. Although this interpersonal approach reduces girls' likelihood of experiencing violence, it also has negative effects on their emotional well-being. Those who choose protective custody find that being in a cell for most of the day is their best bet for staying safe. This choice does not, however, grant them immunity from various forms of violence.

These strategies for navigating detention cannot be understood without careful consideration of the role of the institution and those who work for it. At El Valle Juvenile Detention Facility, jail staff created an environment that encouraged young people to participate in violence and punished those who did not participate in this behavior. Fighting in detention (and the contributions of jail staff to this behavior) is even more alarming when we consider the original offenses that led the girls to detention. Forty of the fifty girls in my study were first incarcerated for nonviolent, drug-related offenses. The offenses that were considered violent almost always began in the girls' homes and were often tied to fighting back against abuse. In other words, fighting was not an issue for girls I studied, until they entered El Valle. Once in detention, however, engaging in fights regularly earned girls more time behind bars. This is important for several reasons. First, the environment that jail staff fostered contributed to this unwanted behavior. Second, this behavior, when replicated outside of El Valle, pushes the girls further and further into the arms of the criminal justice system. The more time that girls spend behind bars, the more likely they are to end up at Legacy Community School, where they experience hypersurveillance and regular police contact. Thus, the cycle reinforces itself. Ultimately, through their behavior, correctional staff directly contradict the stated goal of wraparound services, which is to keep youth out of secure confinement.

While correctional staff can hurt young people in detention, they can also prevent violence. I less frequently observed correctional officers preventing fights. Though infrequent, these instances highlight opportunities to reduce fighting in general. Training staff to avoid praising violent behavior, and encouraging them to instead intervene in a respectful manner, might produce fewer fights. Changing the context of interpersonal interactions can also reduce violence. For example, Artz and Nicholson found that institutions like schools can reduce violence among high-risk girls by "offering a cooperative, encouraging atmosphere that supports the girls' feelings of belonging and connectedness in the program" (2010, 169). In other words, shifting the institutional atmosphere in detention in a way that creates a positive environment can also help reduce violence. This institutional shift is extremely important in every institution young women face, including detention centers and community day schools.

Many of the young women I studied bounced between Legacy and El Valle, and their stories illustrate how girls get caught up in the juncture between the California education system and the penal system. The Recuperation Program provides a useful case study of how wraparound incarceration shapes the trajectories of justice-involved adolescent girls. Unlike other alternative and community day school students, students in the Recuperation Program face the constant presence of law enforcement agents. Their behavior is always under surveillance; as a result, they are continuously at risk of ending up in secure detention.

Academic, interpersonal, gender, and socioeconomic factors also influence girls' experiences at school. For example, the young women in my study were required to make difficult decisions about staying in Legacy or going on the run. These choices and the negative repercussions associated with these decisions would not exist in a traditional school. Most importantly, students in the Recuperation Program are doubly punished for their behavior in the community. The current literature shows that young people are receiving criminal sanctions for things that happen outside of school (Kupchik, 2010; Hirschfield, 2009; Kupchik, 2009). My research shows, however, that probation violations or status offenses in the community committed by Legacy students result not only in time in a detention center but also in punishments within the school setting (such as more time in the Recuperation Program). These findings are significant, since most of the young women in this study were first arrested on the streets and not at school. Their presence in the Recuperation Program, however, led to more arrests or other sanctions that kept them tied to the criminal justice system.

In Legacy generally, and in the Recuperation Class specifically, it is difficult for young people to escape the formal surveillance they experience in detention, which ranges from the probation officer stationed inside their classrooms to random drug testing to supervision on the bus. Students enrolled in these programs are more likely than typical teenagers to be caught and punished for their offenses, possibly even sent to El Valle. The collaboration of multiple state agencies in the form of wraparound services is intended to help students, but the reality, as I noted earlier, looks more like wraparound incarceration. Surveillance and punishment take place at the juncture between these two institutions. This is especially the case in the Recuperation Program.

The limitations of wraparound services are evident in several ways. First, instead of adequately treating students' drug addictions, law enforcement agents are simply placing these students in secure detention. This program also falls short of addressing the external home and community factors that might contribute to students' drug use. These young people might have mental health issues, too, that are not addressed. Drug testing students at will, moreover, pushes them to make rash decisions. All of this is to say that wraparound services in this setting prioritize punishment over protection and rehabilitation. In the eyes of school and detention administrators and practitioners, catching students committing crimes serves as an indicator of success. In other words, they believe that the more behavior they detect and punish, the more they are helping these young people. This assumption created negative consequences for the girls in my study and demonstrates the negative consequences of wraparound incarceration.

Community day schools, the Recuperation Program, probation supervision, and wraparound services are intended to help rehabilitate young people and keep them out of secure detention. Despite these good intentions, most young people in these programs are failing, and they often return to secure detention. Instead of finding themselves on the pathway to success, they find themselves more deeply entrenched in the criminal justice system.

The challenges that some of the young women in my study faced in the detention center and community day school often continued as they struggled to reintegrate into a traditional school. Their mistreatment at traditional schools put them in situations that landed them back in detention. This mistreatment was directly connected to probation, their previous incarceration, and electronic monitoring, all of which are a part of wraparound services intended to keep them out of secure detention. At their new schools, as at Legacy and El Valle, they could not escape the negative effects of wraparound services or the negative label these institutions attached to them. Girls experienced institutional harassment at the hands of teachers and school administrators, and the labels these individuals imposed on them were not related to their actual behavior and academic ability or to the added challenges they faced when returning to a comprehensive school.

This targeting was directly connected to teachers' perceptions of girls' "negative" behavior and general attitude. This behavior included fighting, using drugs, and dressing in provocative attire or other clothes that school officials considered to be related to gang culture often associated with young Latinos and Latinas. The girls' behavior also included verbally challenging the authority of school personnel. In the eyes of education officials, all of these behaviors are problematic and directly connected to Latinas' participation in youth gangs (Vigil, 2008; Rios, 2006; Katz, 1997). Their probation, too, a product of wraparound services, also made these young women a target for school officials. This is consistent with current research that has found that teachers and principals alike tend to go out of their way to punish justice-involved youth for small infractions like being late, missing class, or arguing with teachers or other students (McGrew, 2008; Casella, 2003).

Eventually, the individuals in my study were suspended, expelled, and sent back to Legacy or another form of alternative school. Given the multiple interpersonal and institutional challenges girls faced while attending school, a large portion stopped attending. They made a conscious decision to avoid an institution where they felt uncomfortable, unsafe, and unwanted. At first, this choice worked. Later, however, these young women would be cited for excessive truancy. Importantly, most young women at this point in their path through the criminal justice system were being arrested for violating academic rules. In addition to excessive truancy (a probation violation), the reasons for their arrest included being caught in the community during school hours (a truancy violation) and attempting to return to school after a long absence (trespassing and a truancy violation).

The stigma of wraparound services often hurts youth, and the sudden removal of wraparound support leaves girls feeling lost. My findings reveal an additional shortcoming of wraparound services. First, intensive supervision does not entirely prepare young people for their return to a traditional school. Instead, it creates a sense of institutionalization, so that they return to traditional school with heightened feelings of vulnerability. Nor do wraparound services take into account how the stigma of being incarcerated makes youth targets for interpersonal and institutional harassment. While wraparound services are intended to provide youth with support at home, in detention, at school, and in the community, these services expose girls to added challenges and continued contact with the criminal justice system. In other words, wraparound services did not prepare them to return to a traditional school and actually complicated their transition back to a normal life. Nevertheless, a few girls somehow made the transition.

One way that girls exit criminal pathways is by actively negotiating the constant presence of criminal justice agents in class and, in doing so, undergoing a cognitive shift that allows them to take a positive view of the surveillance they experience. Pregnancy, too, is important in young women's transition away from the criminal justice system (Giordano, Cernkovich, and Rudolph, 2002). Two of the girls I studied discovered that their pregnancies helped them become sober or allowed them to mature. This last finding is consistent with research by other scholars who state that having a child helps young women stay sober and leave criminal pathways (Kreager, Matsueda, and Erosheva, 2010; Benda, 2005). The lack of a stable home, however, meant that becoming pregnant often had a negative effect for the young people in my study. Interestingly, two of the young women became ready for change after experiencing a life in which they were productive, happy, and free from criminal justice agencies. These experiences were key to shaping their desire to leave their criminal pathways.

Getting off probation and finding a safe home were the most important components of successfully leaving the criminal justice system. Two of the young women in my study demonstrate how getting off probation and staying away from wraparound services were more important than experiencing a positive cognitive shift or staying sober. Most importantly, finding a safe home where the young women could avoid the multiple gendered forms of violence they previously had experienced was key to successfully exiting criminal pathways. A safe home doubles as a place where young women can avoid criminalization, and not having a safe haven results in future arrest. This was especially the case for one young woman who willingly returned to secure detention when five months pregnant and after being on the run for multiple months. Her contact with the criminal justice system continued after she gave birth. The case of another girl demonstrates how a shift to a safe and normal home environment can lead young women away from the justice system. These two final points are the most significant for young women attempting to exit criminal pathways.

With this research, I make four central contributions to the current literature on surveillance in schools, feminist criminology, and life course theory. First, investigating the experiences of young Latinas at El Valle Juvenile Detention Facility and Legacy Community School allowed me to identify the multiple processes these young people experienced when navigating the increasingly connected American educational and penal systems. While scholars have long discussed the "school-to-prison pipeline," my work identifies the newest manifestation of this phenomenon. Specifically, what young people may encounter is not a pipeline—that is, not a linear trajectory they follow from school to prison—but a multi-institution, multiagency set of dynamic barriers, through which they can be criminalized and subsequently incarcerated. This process begins long before young women ever set foot in a classroom. In the past, school was often a refuge where youth could briefly escape the challenges in their neighborhoods, and it represented the chance to pursue some form of economic mobility. Now, however, it is becoming increasingly difficult in almost every setting for all youth to avoid contact with the criminal justice system. This is especially true at school, where girls are now more susceptible to criminalization than ever before (Winn, 2011; Winn 2010). My findings shed light on a new dynamic juncture that exists between juvenile detention centers and community day schools like Legacy. As institutional partnerships such as this one increase, a growing number of young people will be funneled into institutions of confinement. This is especially true for poor young men and women of color, who disproportionately attend community day schools.

My research also allowed me to uncover the hidden consequences of wraparound services, a phenomenon affecting large segments of young men and women in California. Wraparound services are more pronounced in the Recuperation Class at Legacy than in any other institution encountered by the youth I studied. The partnership between Legacy Community School and El Valle Juvenile Detention Facility is key to this relationship. Other research in this area has discussed the fact that police officers are now on most school campuses in the United States. My work adds to this discussion by showing how the criminal justice system has become incorporated into the administrative and economic structure of public education. As schools continue to struggle financially and experience numerous budget cuts, they will continue to look for new forms of support. My findings suggest that more schools may begin to seek out economic help from the criminal justice system, whose resources continue to expand (McGrew, 2008). Wraparound services—one product of this financial relationship—do not help keep young people out of secure detention.

My work also contributes to empirical and theoretical research on the life course and criminal desistance. Most research on the life course focuses on criminal desistance and the deviant trajectories of young men and boys (Sampson and Laub, 1993; Sampson and Laub, 1992). Departing from this work, I have focused on the criminal pathways of young women. Like Giordano, Cernkovich, and Rudolph (2002), I have identified key turning points that help young women leave a life in crime, especially cognitive shifts away from crime, locating a stable home, and leaving formal proba-tion. I have also shed light on the racialized, socioeconomic, and gender-specific challenges Latinas face when attempting to leave a life of crime. This is important since Latinas and Latinos continue to be understudied in life course research and in the study of crime as a whole (Garcia, 2012; Dietrich, 1998; Segura, 1993; Soto, 1986; Fox, 1983). My finding that exiting the formal probation system is a key component to avoiding criminal pathways speaks to other research on formal labeling by the criminal justice system (Sampson and Laub, 1993; Hagan and Palloni, 1990b).

My findings also contribute new knowledge to scholars' understandings of life behind bars. Theoretical work on prisons suggests that detention centers attempt to control individuals and strip them of their individuality (Foucault, 1978; Foucault, 1977; Goffman, 1968). According to these understandings of life behind bars, such institutions control every facet of life in this space. In contrast, I found that girls use their modest power to negotiate potential threats and to keep themselves safe.

My book as a whole contributes to studies at the intersection of race, class, gender, and crime. Young people are punished in racialized, gendered, and class-specific ways in every institution. At home, young women are punished for violating traditional expectations regarding gender and culture for young Latinas. Ironically, this behavior is often connected to the abuse they experience at the hands of their guardians. This punishment continues when girls enter El Valle Juvenile Detention Facility. In this space, girls quickly learn they are responsible for their own well-being, and that ensuring personal safety requires fighting and establishing a reputation as someone who is willing and able to assert her will via a physical clash. Girls in detention, however, find themselves punished by correctional guards, who view fighting as unbecoming of young Latinas. In this space, guards simultaneously reward girls for fighting and punish them for participating in the same behavior. At Legacy Community School, as at their home schools, girls discover that adults' perceptions of them as gender violators, and the punishments associated with these violations, are inescapable. These girls are marked as justice-involved youth and labeled "bad" girls who have no place in school. The challenges young women encounter in these settings are further complicated by their various intersecting identities. As other research suggests, this new extension of mass incarceration punishes youth in gendered, racialized, and class-specific ways.

One theme in the literature on youth and the criminal justice system centers on unintended consequences. Rios (2011) has found that, in Oakland, California, well-intentioned adults and community centers that take funding from criminal justice agencies unintentionally criminalize young men. In this same vein, Paik (2011) states that juvenile drug courts in Miami, Florida, that were created to help youth with drug dependency issues often differentially punish young people along gender and racialized lines. This in turn reinforces current inequality in the criminal justice system. My own research similarly demonstrates how the criminal justice system adversely affects young people when attempting to keep them away from detention centers. Scholars can also see the effects of the increasing material and economic connections between community centers and the criminal justice system. This phenomenon merits further investigation. Given that several cities in California, and cities in various parts of the country, are establishing similar relationships between their educational and criminal-justice institutions, I am confident that my findings also speak to the experiences of girls in other parts of the state and in other cities across the United States. Although this study did not focus specifically on boys, my findings also apply to male youth inside schools and detention centers. It is nevertheless important to note that these findings specifically address some of the racialized, socioeconomic, and gendered challenges that Latinas encounter.

After spending six months attempting to gain access to El Valle, I was finally going to enter my new field site. As I walked through the concrete corridors and passed the steel doors that secured the facility, I wondered how my research participants would react to my presence in their unit. Before reaching the girls' unit, I arrived at the final door that stood between me and my research participants, pressed the button and waited for a correctional officer to "buzz me in." The classroom where I would spend much of my time was on my right. Ms. Sanchez, the teacher, invited me to sit down before her students arrived. As the girls began filing into the classroom, they all gave me curious looks. Since I was the only man in the room, I imagine it was impossible for them not to notice my presence in class.

As I considered how to introduce myself, Emma, a five-foot-eight, six-months-pregnant Latina adolescent with tattoos on her face and a long scar on her left arm, asked, "Who is this man in the classroom?" Her question made me smile, and Ms. Sanchez asked me, "Would like to introduce yourself?" I stood up in front of the class and said, "Hello, and thank you for inviting me into your class. I know I am a man, and men suck sometimes." The class laughed, and I began to tell them about myself and my family, who had immigrated from central Mexico after the collapse of the economy in the 1980s. I also mentioned my experiences as a high school dropout and former drug user, and I discussed my current and future research. When I asked the students if they had any questions, someone asked me how old I was.

I avoided the question, saying only: "I am a good age." After this, I sat down and the teacher began her lesson.

Emma and her question, "who is this man," was typical of my experiences while doing research with incarcerated young women. The young people (and staff) often questioned my motives for being present, particularly since I was the only man in the unit. Here, I discuss the unique challenges I had as a man doing research with young women. By far, the biggest challenge was convincing young women and staff that I was not a predatory person, a challenge made especially difficult given the previous victimization these young women had experienced and the long-standing history of institutional male figures exploiting women behind bars (Pasko, 2010; Owen, 2003; Rasche, 2003; Burton-Rose, 2003). Convincing them of my intentions required that I avoid sexualized conversations and behaviors with my research participants. It also included reporting improper behavior between adults in the facility and the young people who were housed in this detention center.

Before getting to that, however, it will be helpful to begin with a brief discussion of reflexivity and how my own personal biography and experiences shaped the research process.

FROM "AT-RISK" YOUTH TO ACADEMIC: A NOTE ON REFLEXIVITY

Being reflexive and considering one's own identities and experiences is a key aspect of the research process (Rios, 2011; Jones, 2010; Finlay, 2002; Zavella, 1993). Reflexivity has always intrigued me, since it allows me to connect my personal experience of oppression to the research process. It also allows me to explain how inequality shaped my life and the lives of individuals in my community and communities similar to my own.

My research on the intersections of race, class, gender, sexuality, and crime, as well as on the increased fusion of educational and penal institutions, is directly informed by my personal experiences. My parents came to California in 1982 to work grueling ten-to-twelve-hour days in Los Angeles's textile factories and automotive repair industry. Upon their arrival, they were forced to work long hours not only to support our immediate family but also to aid our extended family in Mexico. Given these economic constraints, we lived in a predominantly working-class Mexican enclave in Pasadena, California. While Pasadena has a reputation as a wealthy community that hosts the annual Rose Parade and Rose Bowl, we lived in an area with working-class and working-poor families. In my neighborhood we had few academic role models; the people with criminal records outnumbered those with college degrees. As a young person I always expected to join the ranks of automotive repair workers, like my father. For me and for other young people growing up in these communities, higher education and the thought of leaving our neighborhoods seemed like little more than pipe dreams. Put simply, college and upward mobility were not for us.

These feelings are often exacerbated by young people's experiences at school. As a high school freshman I was searched by campus police with drug-sniffing dogs, frisked during class, and thrown on the hood of a campus police car for skating—treatment that was and is common for young men of color in my neighborhood. While other, predominantly white, middle-class students in my school were admitted to college preparatory courses, I was funneled into classes like "math topics," where I learned how to balance a checkbook and calculate sales tax on grocery purchases. I, like many of the students in my research, experienced the school-to-prison pipeline and police mistreatment firsthand. During this time I began to consume alcohol, amphetamines, and psychotropic drugs, and my performance in school plummeted. After years of police and teacher maltreatment, an education that seemed completely irrelevant, and my increased drug use, I dropped out of high school at sixteen years of age.

Eventually, I enrolled in Options for Youth, a continuation school where "at-risk" students fulfill California's compulsory education laws. Here, away from some of the negative influences in my life and surrounded by caring instructors, I heard people say for the first time in my young life: "You are smart, and you should go to college." At this new school, I was able to meet and exceed academic expectations by working independently to complete a year's worth of high school units in just one semester. The following academic term I returned to my home school and became the first person in my family to graduate from high school. I enrolled in Pasadena Community College and later Grossmont College. Previously, my parents had seen me as an underachiever and thought I would be part of the unskilled labor force. Their perceptions of me transformed into a sense of pride and hope, since I would attain the education and professional positions they never achieved. After many years I earned a PhD and became an academic, teacher, and professional researcher. My experiences in the educational and criminal justice systems, both as a researcher and as a target of these systems, have allowed me to gain a unique perspective, which I used when conducting this research.

GETTING IN

My interest in working with incarcerated young women began in 2008. During that time, I was a master's student in the sociology department at San Diego State University doing research on the experiences of teachers who worked inside male juvenile detention centers along the United States–Mexico border. I was conducting a final interview with a white man in his midthirties. We sat in a loud donut shop in San Diego, and he told me about teaching in detention. Toward the end of our interview, I asked him, "Are there any questions you thought I would ask you but I didn't?" He replied, "Yes, you didn't ask me anything about gender. Teaching boys and teaching girls have their own sets of challenges and rewards. You should think about that." I left the shop thinking about my interviewee. I decided to explore this issue when I started my graduate studies in the sociology department at the University of California, Santa Barbara. In a sense, this moment was the beginning of this larger study and my interest in doing research with incarcerated girls. Before this (and while blinded by my male privilege), I had not considered working with young women.

Gaining access to El Valle Juvenile Detention Facility was a difficult and slow process. Getting in was the first and largest hurdle in the research process. The initial fieldwork for this project began in a research methods course that I took as a first-year graduate student. My former instructor and mentor, Nikki Jones, told the seminar, "Go find a research site, and don't come back without one." I began to visit the parking lots of nearby youth detention facilities, sitting in my car for hours, taking field notes, and observing the comings and goings of individuals entering these spaces. I then contacted the principals of correctional schools in the area and introduced myself via email.[1] I explained who I was and my (initial) interest in understanding how girls negotiate attending school behind bars.

One principal returned my message and invited me to fill out paperwork to become a volunteer at El Valle Juvenile Detention Facility. After four months, three background checks, one fingerprinting, and several orientations, I was allowed to meet with the principal inside the facility. This administrator seemed skeptical of my intentions. He asked, "Why this facility?" during our meeting. I explained that his was the only facility willing to meet with me. I told him that my goal was to help the girls as much as possible while I visited. I also told him I would help by tutoring the youth at the facility and participating in any activities that he believed would facilitate their success. I explained that I would volunteer as many hours as I spent doing research. We also discussed my own troubled past.[2] Finally, I explained that my goal was to get every girl at the facility into a college classroom. After this meeting, he agreed to let me conduct research at this site. I later expanded my work to include Legacy Community School. I believe my desire to help these young people enabled my entrée into the facility. This agreement made me one of just a handful of researchers who have done work in institutions of confinement in the United States, and especially in California, since the 1980s; even fewer have gained access to juvenile detention centers (Bickel 2010).

This research is even more significant given that I am a man doing research with incarcerated young women. Few men have access to women in correctional facilities, largely for the women's own protection. Women in corrections have been sexually abused by men since women first entered secure confinement (Tapia, 2010; Rasche, 2003; Burton-Rose, 2003). This type of sexual misconduct continues today, and news reports of male correctional officers assaulting incarcerated women are a common occurrence (Tapia, 2010; Pasko, 2010; Owen, 2003). Given the pattern of sexual abuse inside these institutions, administrators in the 1970s started restricting men's contact with women who were then behind bars (Rasche, 2003); these restrictions continue today. In my case, I believe my desire to help these young people, and my willingness to volunteer my time, helped facilitate my access to the facility. I also believe I was granted access because of a group of compassionate educators and criminal justice practitioners who were interested in the well-being of the young people in their custody.

Once these administrators allowed me to enter the facility, I began the lengthy process of applying for and attaining approval to study human subjects. I began the human-subjects review process by listing basic information about my field sites and subjects. This information included the scope of my study, the subjects I intended to work with, copies of consent forms, and information about how I would protect my participants' identities. I then needed permission from the head administrator at El Valle, the principal from Plazo Correctional School, and Legacy Community School. Securing these permissions was key to receiving human-subjects approval, often the most difficult part of doing research in detention centers. After this, I was required to find an advocate for my participants who worked in detention. This was an adult whom the girls could speak to if they felt uncomfortable or concerned with my presence or with any component of the study. The director of a nonprofit organization in the detention center agreed to serve in this role during my project.

Once these components were set in place, I needed to draft a consent form for the youth in my study. Both the young women and their guardians needed to sign the form if they were to participate in an individual interview. For young people in the foster care system, the detention center operated as the caretaker of record and agreed to consent on their behalf. For young people who lived at home, I was required to send a letter home and wait two weeks for a response. If the parents denied permission by phone, email, or letter, I did not include the child in my study. This final part of acquiring consent was clearly not ideal. However, it was extremely difficult to contact participants' parents directly.

After beginning fieldwork, I quickly learned that the principal and the other teachers in this setting were in a unique and often challenging position. Plazo Correctional School exists inside the larger detention center. Unlike traditional schools, which are usually under the direct supervision of a centralized school district, schools like this one function under the auspices of both the local law enforcement agency and the local school district. Although in some ways these schools operate like almost any other school, they differ in that they must adhere to the rules, regulations, and authority of the law enforcement agency that controls the facility. Classrooms here are located inside the unit where youth are held. Because of this, it takes less than one minute for students to walk out of their cells and into class. Officers are in charge of supervising students throughout the institution and dealing with disciplinary issues such as fights and aggressive behavior in the class-room. I noted a constant tension between school staff and correctional offic-ers at this site. The source of the tension may have been the conflict between the more altruistic goals of school staff as compared to the goals of correc-tional officers. This may also explain why the principal of the school was receptive to my desire to volunteer at his school. Such tensions between cor-rectional staff and school employees are common at other research sites.

SEXUAL ABUSE, HEGEMONIC MASCULINITY, AND PRIVILEGE IN THE RESEARCH PROCESS

Before discussing my experiences in the field, it is important to address the intense forms of sexual abuse that justice-involved young women encounter in their everyday lives. Other scholars have found, as I did, that young women in the criminal justice system have historically experienced sexual abuse before their incarceration (Pasko, 2008; Belknap, Holsinger, and Dunn, 1997). Other feminist criminologists have long identified sexual abuse as a precursor for young women's offending and future incarceration (Pasko, 2010; Pasko, 2008; Mc-Daniels-Wilson and Belknap, 2008; Belknap, 2006; Bloom, Owen, and Covington, 2004; Bloom, Owen, Deschenes, and Rosen-baum, 2002). Several studies have also documented how young women who were sexually abused at home (often by family members) were later arrested after they ran away to escape this mistreatment (Chesney-Lind, 2006; Chesney-Lind and Pasko, 2004). A more recent study found that rates of sexual abuse continue to be disproportionately high for incarcerated women compared to incarcerated men. For example, one survey of four hundred incarcerated women in Ohio found that 70 percent of participants experi-enced sexual abuse before being incarcerated (Mc-Daniels-Wilson and Belknap, 2008).

Justice-involved young women as a whole often experience some form of sexual abuse when returning home after being incarcerated, especially if they chose to flee this abuse in their place of residence (Mc-Daniels-Wilson and Belknap, 2008; Schaffner, 2006). Once on the street, these young peo-ple are often forced to make a difficult decision: stay on the street and face multiple forms of gendered violence, or participate in "survival sex" after leaving home. This term has been used to describe the behavior of women who exchange sex for money, drugs, or shelter as a means of daily survival (Shannon, Bright, Gibson, and Tyndall, 2007). Survival sex places young women at a heightened risk for sexually transmitted infections, as well as for poverty, substance abuse, and additional forms of physical, sexual, and psychological mistreatment (Shannon, Bright, Gibson, and Tyndall, 2007; Chesney-Lind and Pasko, 2004). Participating in survival sex also increases young women's likelihood of being arrested and subsequently incarcerated. For young people in this study and other justice-involved youth, trading sex for a place to stay, for food, or for other resources is often their only means of keeping themselves relatively safe once on the streets.

The hypersexualization of these young people and the behaviors they engage in to survive often carry over to their interactions with individuals in the community and behind bars. For example, when discussing the lives of incarcerated girls in California's Bay Area, Schaffner reports that, "while still children, girls in corrections used their youthful appeal to adult male heterosexuality in order to meet their normal childhood needs for food, clothing, shelter, adult guidance, and family love" (2006, 103). When they were largely fending for themselves in adolescence, the young women in my study often depended on how effectively they could exchange their sexuality for safety or other forms of support. This behavior, and their hypersexualization as a whole, carried over to my interactions with my participants. This tendency is extremely relevant to my attempts to avoid discussions with them about dating and sex. The young women's attempts to engage in behaviors that might otherwise be considered "flirting" or "inappropriate" may, in fact, have been related to their view of the best way to ensure their own survival. At the same time, it is important to keep in mind that all forms of young women's expressions of sexuality have historically been criminalized by the juvenile justice system (Chavez-Garcia, 2009; Pasko, 2008; Chesney-Lind and Pasko, 2004).

I also approached my research with an awareness of how hegemonic masculinity operates. *Hegemonic masculinity* refers to a gendered approach that involves the subjugation and exploitation of women in ways that reproduce the domination of certain groups of men (Mayeda and Pasko, 2012; Connell and Messerschmidt, 2005). It is a presentation of self that valorizes men's "high degree of ruthless competition, an inability to express emotions other than anger, an unwillingness to admit weakness or dependency, devaluation of women and all feminine attributes in men, homophobia and so forth" (Kupers, 2005, 716). Schippers builds on Connell's definition of this term, stating, "Hegemonic masculinity ensures male dominance, [and] all men benefit on some level even though most men don't have to be 'on the front lines' or embody hegemonic masculinity" (2007, 88). In other words, hegemonic masculinity is a process that occurs in overt as well as covert and unintended ways.

Given the young women's previous experience of sexual exploitation, I wanted to approach my research in a way that avoided their further victimization. I additionally hoped to limit my own contribution to hegemonic masculinity. I did this in several ways. First, I spent large amounts of time getting to know these young people. I often visited on the weekends or holidays and simply played board games, watched movies, or played basketball. I also participated in their classes and other detention center activities. This helped me build healthy relationships with these young people—for some of them, a new experience. During our conversations and interviews, I checked in with my participants to make sure they were comfortable answering my many questions. I also reminded them that they could skip any questions that made them uncomfortable without any negative consequences. When the issues of sexual abuse came up, I let them know that we could stop the interview at any point. However, most young women wanted to discuss their victimization and negative experiences. I tried to listen empathetically and provided suggestions for how to move forward with their trauma. I also shared my own experiences of victimization as a child and spoke about my own emotions and experiences openly.

Although I tried to avoid hurting or revictimizing these young people, there was no way to guarantee that my questions would not cause them further harm. I did, however, agree to share my work with them, and I told them how to find my research online, even if they could not contact me in person. Thus, I attempted to adopt an approach to doing this work that revolved around trying to find ways to eventually improve these young women's lives while simultaneously attempting to treat the young women with dignity and respect. Ultimately, I wanted to help them, and I attempted to aid them as much as possible during my twenty-four months of fieldwork.

The juvenile justice system has a history of adopting a paternalist and condescending approach to helping young women. For example, Pasko (2008) reports that the criminal justice system adopts a paternalistic approach that "helps" young women by punishing them for low-level offenses. This approach also includes punishing any actual or perceived expression of young women's sexuality (Chavez-Garcia, 2009; Pasko, 2008; Chesney-Lind and Pasko, 2004). I attempted to avoid this pattern of "help" in several ways. For example, I organized workshops that explained how to negotiate the community college system and successfully transfer to a four-year college. We also had group discussions on navigating high school and negotiating life in community day schools. Other days we would have short-story- or poetry-writing workshops. During these group activities, the young people in my study often shared the challenges in their lives and openly discussed their experiences. Some days we would sit and talk about their concerns and questions about life in general or life after incarceration specifically. Along these same lines, I participated in group activities like soccer matches, volleyball games, and any other activities that allowed me to have positive interactions with these youth. My desire to help came from my personal experiences and my hope that these young people would have better lives upon their release. Although it is entirely possible that this "help" replicated the paternalistic treatment of these young people, I attempted to avoid this negative pattern.

During the research process, I also attempted to acknowledge my privilege as a newly middle-class man. While I grew up as a working-class person in a poor, segregated Latino enclave, my education, gender, and class status now allowed me to live a comfortable life. I had somewhere safe to stay, I did not have to worry about being sexually assaulted while walking to my car at night, and I always had money in my checking account. My car also started every time, all the time. I had the privilege of being heard whenever I opened my mouth and the privilege of knowing that people assumed I knew what I was talking about when I spoke. I also knew that my privileged position as a whole encouraged the young women in my study to answer my many questions even if they did not care to speak with me or if they did not want me in the girls' unit at all. Along these same lines, I (as a man) got to design and control almost every aspect of this research project on young incarcerated women. This is especially important, given that these girls would most likely receive no substantial benefit from the work I produced. Finally, I tried to acknowledge the biggest privilege of all, which was my ability to leave the detention center whenever I chose. This was not an option for either the young women in my study or other incarcerated individuals around the globe.

DOING RESEARCH WITH GIRLS

The research process presented several challenges associated with being a man doing research with young women. Understanding how I navigated these challenges is important not only for evaluating my study but also because most discussion of this issue focuses on women's experiences doing fieldwork with men (Vanderbeck, 2005). The central challenge was to convince both the girls and the staff housing them that I was not a predator. Convincing both of these groups was difficult; it was something I continually had to negotiate. I achieved some degree of trust in three central ways: by avoiding discussions about dating and sex, reporting inappropriate behavior by staff, and avoiding physical contact.

During fieldwork, I avoided conversations about dating and rebuffed what might be interpreted as girls' romantic advances. I started off most visits by talking about my partner, whom I later married during the research process. To gain information about my relationship status, young women would often ask questions like: "How old are you?" or "Are you married?" Other girls would compliment my clothing or say, "You smell good." Or they might say, "You look nice today." These comments would often happen after interviews when my participants had shared traumatic events in their lives. When this occurred, I simply ignored these comments or walked away. I captured one such incident in my field notes:

> There is a girl with dark wavy hair that looks to be Pacific Islander. She asks, "Where is your long-sleeve Dickies [referring to one of my shirts]?" I reply, "Its probably dirty," and I walk back toward the other side of the unit. I walk past a Latina correctional officer who witnessed the exchange, and she says, "Esa cabrona esta safada. Se esta siendo mensa" [That girl has a screw loose. She is acting stupid]. Believing the girl was trying to flirt with me, I chuckled at her comment and walked into one of the classrooms inside the unit.

This exchange demonstrates one of the strategies I used to avoid conversations and behavior that I felt were "inappropriate" for a professional researcher doing fieldwork with underage women. In this case, both the correctional officer and I felt this young woman was attempting to flirt with me. When I picked up on this behavior, I walked away, removing myself from the situation altogether. Once the girls in the jail became aware of this pattern, they often avoided this type of conversation. Other times, young women intervened on my behalf when overhearing inappropriate comments by saying things like: "He is twenty-five and married." Such comments would end these sexualized exchanges and girls' inquiries about my dating status. While situations like these might seem like simply the romantic advances of young women or a young person with a crush, it is important to keep in mind how often young incarcerated women have had to depend on their sexuality and sexual appeal to survive. I was not alone in facing these challenges; they are common to men doing research with young women (Okamoto, 2002).

Avoiding conversations related to sex was also a challenge during formal activities. For example, I often volunteered in the classroom or with a local nonprofit that provided gender-specific programming inside the detention center. The nonprofit facilitator asked me to take part in a role-playing exercise. I was partnered with sixteen-year-old Marianna, who was three months pregnant. The scenario involved a boyfriend trying to convince his partner to consume alcohol and have intercourse. This made the facilitator, the correctional officer who was present, and myself uncomfortable. I defused the situation by quickly volunteering to play the part of the young woman rejecting the young man's sexual advances. During the exercise, Marianna attempted to get me to drink alcohol, and I replied, "I don't want to, because I am not safe when I drink." The exercise ended without incident, and I went to speak with the correctional officer after the event. I told her, "That made me a bit nervous." She agreed, and we began to discuss another issue as the girls finished their meeting. This case was only one example of how I negotiated avoiding sensitive topics and situations during the fieldwork process.

During fieldwork I was also hyperaware of where I focused my attention. I often stared at the ground when my participants engaged in behaviors that accentuated their bodies. For example, I often looked at the walls or the floor when girls stretched or played soccer. I attempted to make this obvious, to avoid making my participants uncomfortable. I recorded this in a field note: "The project is going well. I feel really comfortable with the girls; and I am afraid I am getting too comfortable, so I am going to try to distance myself. During the interview Feliz was scratching her chest and adjusting her bra, and I looked at the floor; and I did that every time she was fidgeting. I don't want to send her or anyone else the wrong signal." This field note reflects my general reactions and thinking during the research process. I regularly kept in mind how my behavior (including my gaze) affected my participants' perceptions of me as a man doing research with girls. I was especially cognizant of this given the sexual abuse these young people have experienced and the legacy of male institutional actors exploiting incarcerated women.

REPORTING INAPPROPRIATE BEHAVIOR

Part of convincing the girls I was not predatory, and part of not contributing to hegemonic masculinity, involved reporting inappropriate behavior by jail staff and other personnel. Given the history of men abusing women in detention, this facility did not allow men to permanently work in the girls' unit. Men were, however, allowed to work there temporarily or to volunteer in the facility. During a routine interview with my primary respondent (Feliz), she shared that a priest in the facility had caressed her arm and told her, "You are a very pretty girl." I found this especially alarming since, just before this inappropriate contact, Feliz had shared with the priest her experience of being drugged and raped by a group of boys. After she shared this information about the priest, she asked me not to mention it to anyone. I eventually contacted the human-subjects review board before I reported the incident to administrators at the facility. I also met with Feliz the next day to discuss what happened and to tell her that I was required to report the incident. I reassured her that everything would be fine, and that the detention center would do a formal investigation. I also assured her that she did the right thing by telling me, since this priest could be hurting other people. Feliz initially felt uncomfortable with this investigation, especially because she had been raped in the past and no one had believed her. After a formal investigation, El Valle banned the priest from returning to the facility. I also continued to check in with Feliz after this incident ended.

After this, jail staff began to be more open to my presence and also started giving me suggestions for my research and sharing their experiences as correctional officers. One of Feliz's friends also approached me afterward and said, "Thank you for reporting that thing. It was keeping me up at night." Part of convincing girls and staff that I was not predatory involved reporting incidents such as these. Although events of this type were rare in this facility, I believe my actions signaled to others that I was concerned with the well-being of the young people in my research.

AVOIDING PHYSICAL CONTACT

One of the biggest challenges of doing research with young women in detention involved avoiding physical contact. This detention center, like most facilities, has a no-contact policy. This means that there is to be no physical contact between institutional actors and people being housed. This requirement was particularly challenging for me, since I was often the only man these young women saw and the focal point of their attention during my time in the facility. Given these two facts, I regularly had to avoid girls' attempts to participate in friendly physical contact. This contact often involved attempts to hug me or pat me on the back. These young people, like most young people, craved healthy physical contact. The institutional space, the age difference, and my gender, however, complicated such platonic exchanges.

Avoiding hugs was particularly difficult. These exchanges often came as a surprise during the fieldwork process. For example, during a kickball game, Feliz ran up and grabbed a ball I caught. While she was doing this she placed her head on my shoulder and gave me a hug. One of the correctional officers noticed this and called her over immediately. I ignored the event and continued to play, pretending it had not happened. After the game, I thanked the correctional officer for her intervention; she said, "Yeah, I told Feliz she can't be doing that, because she can get you in trouble." She then said not to worry about it, because Feliz "is like that" with all the staff members. Later in the day, however, one of the correctional officers approached a teacher who worked in the facility and said, "Hey, you better talk to your boy, because everybody saw Feliz hug him." While the correctional officer I had spoken with reassured me everything was fine, another officer interpreted my behavior as inappropriate. Given this, I also spoke with Feliz and reminded her that, while I care about the well-being of everyone in detention, it was important to avoid contact so as not to send mixed signals to people at the facility.

Since avoiding physical exchanges was a constant challenge, I developed a set of strategies to discourage the girls from participating in this behavior. First, staff members suggested that I give enthusiastic young people "air hugs," which involved pretending to embrace one of them. This did not work, however, because some enthusiastic young people would simply hug me anyway. I also began to vocally discourage participants from hugging me or patting me on the back. For example, during one incident, seventeen-year-old Cathy said, "I have to go to the bathroom," and patted me on the back as she walked by and attempted to give me a hug. I said, "Hey, you have to ask before you do that," and she said, "No, I don't!" and began to laugh. I turned to a teacher who witnessed this incident and said, "I try to keep my distance because I don't want to send mixed signals," and the teacher said, "Yeah, I know what you mean." When Cathy returned from the bathroom, she attempted to hug me again. This time, I took a step back and extended my closed fist to fist-bump, which is a common greeting among young people. Both speaking to institutional actors about how I was trying to avoid physical contact with my participants, and speaking to girls directly about the issue, were strategies that I used to avoid physical contact and to create healthy boundaries between my research participants and myself.

Creating boundaries between staff members and myself was challenging, too. For example, the correctional officers who worked in the girls' unit were almost all Latina women from working-class backgrounds. These correctional staff and I shared a similar upbringing and cultural experiences, and we were close in age. Given this, they would occasionally invite me to social events, saying things like: "We are going to happy hour after work. You should come hang out. O teva a pegar to vieja [Or will your old lady hit you]?" I often rebuffed such invitations by letting these staff members know I had a lot of work to do, or by informing them I had plans with my partner. I had similar experiences with the educational staff.

Most teachers were white and middle class, and they often probed my relationship status and regularly invited me to "hang out." I avoided most of these events too. I did attend the birthday party of the teacher who became my primary respondent, but I avoided drinking alcohol and brought my partner along. Ms. Sanchez often shared her life events with me, and our relationship felt very friendly. After a volunteer event, she invited me to see her new home, and she let me know that she had a friend over as well. I nervously agreed to see her new apartment. As we entered the apartment, I said hello to her friend, who was sitting in the living room and who was to join us for lunch. I stood in the living room nervously, at which point Ms. Sanchez invited me to see her bedroom. I hesitantly walked upstairs, and she asked me, "What do you think?" and stood in front of me. I said, "It looks good. I'm going to get some water downstairs." After this event, I did not join any other meetings outside of the facility. This experience was also clearly influenced by my privilege as a man and my perception of this teacher, who was a petite (and in my opinion nonthreatening) woman. Unlike women, who constantly deal with the threat of sexual assault, when I entered this space I did not have to fear for my well-being. I quickly realized, however, that entering her home was a bad idea, whether she was attempting to engage me in a romantic encounter or not.

Getting access to the facility that would be my field site was the biggest hurdle during the research process. Once in, however, my participants' gender and my own constantly forced me to consider where I looked, how I carried myself, what I said, and which conversations I chose to acknowledge. No doubt most women have to consider these issues on a constant basis. But given my gender (and privilege), creating healthy boundaries was challenging and an ongoing process that was always in the back of my mind.

Discussions about young women's behavior in detention and upon their release need to be couched in the context of the women's previous abuse and their limited opportunities. While I personally found young women's sexual advances uncomfortable, this behavior is linked to previous abuse and techniques for survival that they have learned. Young women regularly express their sexuality in various ways, and the simple expression of this sexuality should not necessarily make anyone uncomfortable. In the context of secure detention, however, the boundary between healthy sexuality and what one scholar has called "their survival-oriented or abuse-triggered preoccupation with male sexual desire" can be difficult to identify (Schaffner, 2006, 107). Given that young justice-involved women may have been abused at nearly every point in their lives, researchers need to be cognizant of how this might influence the research process.

TABLE 1.

Participant Information

Name	Age	Race	Socioeconomic Status	Violent Offense	Attended Community School	Gang Affiliated	Previously Incarcerated	Age First Incarcerated	Interview	Focus Group	Shadowed
Addie	16	White	Low	N/A	Yes	No	4	N/A	No	Yes	Yes
Alexis	14	Latina	Low	Yes	Yes	Yes	7	12	Yes	Yes	Yes
Alice	16	White	Low	No	Yes	No	4	N/A	No	Yes	No
Allison	19	Latina	Low	N/A	Yes	N/A	3	N/A	No	Yes	Yes
Amber	18	Latina	Low	No	No	No	2	18	Yes	Yes	No
Angie	17	Latina	Low	N/A	N/A	N/A	7	N/A	No	Yes	No
Anita	15	Asian	Low	Yes	No	No	2	14	Yes	Yes	No
Annabelle	17	Latina	Low	Yes	No	Yes	19	13	Yes	Yes	No
Aracely	19	Latina	Low	No	Yes	Yes	19	13	Yes	No	No
Ashley	18	White	Low	N/A	Yes	No	N/A	N/A	No	Yes	No
Betty	16	Black	Low	N/A	Yes	No	3	N/A	No	Yes	Yes
Bonita	17	Latina	Middle	Yes	Yes	Yes	6	14	Yes	Yes	Yes
Brittany	15	White	Low	No	Yes	No	6	14	Yes	No	No
Cathy	17	Latina	Low	N/A	Yes	No	5	N/A	No	No	Yes

(continued)

TABLE 1.

(continued)

Name	Age	Race	Socioeconomic Status	Violent Offense	Attended Community School	Gang Affiliated	Previously Incarcerated	Age First Incarcerated	Interview	Focus Group	Shadowed
Crystal	14	Latina	Low	No	Yes	No	3	13	Yes	Unknown	No
Debby	14	Latina	Low	No	No	Yes	3	13	Yes	No	No
Denise	17	Latina	Low	No	Yes	Yes	5	14	Yes	Yes	Yes
Destiny	18	Latina	Low	No	Yes	Yes	17	12	Yes	No	No
Eve	16	White	Low	N/A	N/A	N/A	7	N/A	No	Yes	No
Feliz	17	Latina	Middle	No	Yes	Yes	5	16	Yes	Yes	No
Haley	18	White	Low	No	N/A	No	N/A	17	Yes	Yes	No
Hanna	16	Latina	Low	No	Yes	N/A	2	15	No	Yes	No
Jackie	15	Latina	Low	No	Yes	No	4	14	Yes	Yes	No
Jennifer	15	Latina	N/A	N/A	N/A	N/A	1	N/A	No	No	No
Jenny	18	Latina	Low	No	Yes	No	4	12	Yes	No	Yes
Juliana	18	Latina	Low	Yes	Yes	Yes	3	17	Yes	No	No
Karen	17	Latina	Low	No	Yes	No	12	16	Yes	Yes	No
Katrina	17	Latina	Low	Yes	Yes	No	8	15	Yes	No	Yes
Kim	17	White	Low	N/A	Yes	Yes	3	N/A	No	Yes	Yes
Lane	17	White	Low	No	Yes	No	4	N/A	Yes	No	No

Name	Age	Ethnicity	Class								
Leticia	16	Latina	Low	N/A	Yes	N/A	N/A	N/A	No	No	Yes
Mari	15	Latina	Low	No	Yes	No	5	14	Yes	No	Yes
Maria	18	Latina	Low	No	Yes	No	12	15	Yes	Yes	No
Mariana	16	Latina	Low	Yes	Yes	Yes	2	14	Yes	Yes	No
Martha	17	Latina	Low	N/A	Yes	Yes	N/A	N/A	No	Yes	Yes
Mary	19	Native American	Low	No	Yes	No	6	16	Yes	No	No
Mary Jane	15	Latina	Low	Yes	Yes	No	2	15	Yes	Yes	No
Patty	16	Latina	Low	N/A	N/A	N/A	4	N/A	No	No	Yes
Rain	15	Latina	Low	No	Yes	N/A	N/A	N/A	No	No	Yes
Rasta	15	White	Low	No	Yes	No	6	13	Yes	Yes	No
Ray	17	Latina	Low	No	Yes	Yes	N/A	14	Yes	Yes	No
Rene	18	Latina	Low	N/A	N/A	Yes	4	N/A	No	Yes	No
Sammy	18	Latina	Low	No	No	Yes	3	N/A	No	Yes	No
Sandra	15	Latina	Low	No	No	Yes	8	13	Yes	No	No
Sarah	16	White	Low	No	Yes	No	4	N/A	No	Yes	No
Shannon	18	White	Low	No	Yes	No	2	17	Yes	No	No
Star	17	Latina	Low	No	No	No	2	16	Yes	Yes	No
Vidi	17	Latina	Low	Yes	N/A	Yes	4	N/A	No	Yes	No
Virginia	16	Latina	Low	Yes	Yes	Yes	1	13	Yes	No	No
Whitney	16	White	Middle	No	Yes	No	2	15	Yes	Yes	No

TABLE 2.

Age and Location of the Subject at First Arrest

Name	Age First Arrested	Location
Alexis	12	Home
Amber	18	Street
Anita	14	Street
Annabelle	13	School
Aracely	13	Home
Bonita	14	Home
Brittany	14	Street
Crystal	13	Street
Debby	13	Street
Denise	14	Street
Destiny	12	Street
Feliz	16	School
Haley	17	Street
Jackie	14	School
Jenny	12	School
Juliana	17	Street
Karen	16	Home
Katrina	15	Street
Lane	N/A	Street
Mari	14	Street
Maria	15	Street
Mariana	14	Street
Mary	16	Street
Mary Jane	15	Street
Rasta	13	Home
Ray	14	Street
Sandra	13	Street
Shannon	17	Home
Virginia	13	Home
Whitney	15	Home

INTRODUCTION

1. This is not the institution's actual name.

2. The names of all people discussed in my study are pseudonyms.

3. None of the schools mentioned in this book have been identified by their real names.

4. Rios's (2011) "youth control complex" also informs my conceptualization of wraparound incarceration. The young men in his study found themselves in situations where adults criminalized their behavior and style on a daily basis. "This ubiquitous criminalization is the youth control complex, a system in which schools, police, probation officers, families, community centers, the media, businesses, and other institutions systematically treat young people's everyday behaviors as criminal activity." Rios argues that, by the time youth in Oakland, California, formally entered the penal system, many of these young men were already caught in a spiral of hypercriminalization and punishment. In contrast, I focus on the experiences of young women before, during, and after their detention. My study provides an in-depth analysis of young people's experiences at home and in the detention center, community day school, and traditional school. These experiences are directly shaped by the criminal justice system and wraparound services.

5. Several other theoretical frameworks influenced my research process. For example, Garland (1990) advocates treating punishment as a social institution and believes that viewing punishment as such allows scholars to look at the complexities and multifaceted nature of punishment. In this book and during the research process, I attempted to follow this suggestion by uncovering new "complexities" of punishment and surveillance. Along the same lines, Garland (1990) and other scholars (cf. Muñiz, 2015; Rios, 2011; Davis, 2003; James, 1996;

Foucault, 1978) advocate understanding penal systems as expressions of state power. While this study does not provide a large theoretical or empirical framework for analyzing state violence, I have attempted to provide a microanalysis of new forms of surveillance and punishment, which are imposed by the state and are a type of institutional oppression.

The work of scholars in critical pedagogy has also influenced my research. Freire, for instance, might argue that the community day schools and correctional schools in my study encourage teachers to embrace the "banking" method of education, in which students are treated as passive, empty receptacles to be filled by the all-knowing instructors. This approach to teaching "leads the students to memorize mechanically the narrated content[,] . . . which the students patiently receive, memorize, and repeat" (1970, 72). Freire and other critical pedagogy scholars call for a dialogical approach to learning that asks teachers and students to share their experiences and knowledge with one another. Dialogical learning emphasizes critical thought and encourages students to critique their reality to find ways of changing the world individually and collectively (Darder, 2002). By relinquishing their oppressive role in "banking" education, instructors can begin to create solidarity with their students by helping them understand how they have been taken advantage of and cheated (Freire, 1970). Most importantly, dialogical teaching requires instructors to teach with compassion and love. In examining this study, it is important to consider both how the education that students receive fits into the banking model, and the unique challenges teachers encounter in these settings.

6. Status offenses are activities or behaviors that are classified as "criminal" by law enforcement agencies only when someone is underage (Chesney-Lind and Shelden, 2014). In many states, including California, parents can ask to have their children arrested for various status offenses, or officers can arrest young people whom they suspect of committing a crime (Champion, 2010). In either case, police usually do not need physical evidence to arrest and detain a minor.

7. All background on the community day schools program comes from California Department of Education, "Community Day Schools Program Summary," last reviewed December 2, 2015, www.cde.ca.gov/sp/eo/cd/summarycds.asp.

8. Correctional officers refused my request for formal interviews. Most of the officers feared reprisal from facility administrators or supervisors. However, several spoke with me off the record, and their insights informed my research.

1. TROUBLE IN THE HOME, AND FIRST CONTACT WITH THE CRIMINAL JUSTICE SYSTEM

1. According to Smith (2003), the category of first-generation Latinos refers to individuals born outside the United States. Second-generation status is

accorded to people born in the United States who have at least one parent born outside the country. Third-generation Latinos and all other subsequent generations are those who have two U.S.-born parents who were themselves born in the United States.

2. A small number of young women in my study lived with friends; however, most of these living arrangements did not last very long. My participants who lived with friends often struggled with increased drug abuse and the potential for victimization by men who lived in the same home with, or who otherwise knew, their friends. Given these circumstances, most girls chose to live with a romantic partner or live on the streets.

3. LEGACY COMMUNITY SCHOOL AND THE NEW FACE OF ALTERNATIVE EDUCATION

1. This information comes from California Legislative Analyst's Office (1995), Juvenile crime—outlook for California, part 5, www.lao.ca.gov/1995/050195_juv_crime/kkpart5.aspx.

2. This information comes from California Legislative Analyst's Office (2007), California's criminal justice system: A primer, www.lao.ca.gov/2007/cj_primer/cj_primer_013107.aspx.

3. Sexual harassment is a pervasive issue facing young women and especially young women of color living in urban areas (Miller, 2008). In her research on Black girls living in urban areas, Miller found that young women who attend alternative schools are often susceptible to sexual harassment before, during, and after school. I found a similar pattern in my own work.

APPENDIX

1. By "correctional schools" I am referring to the schools that exist inside juvenile detention centers.

2. My disciplinary background has also shaped my view of this institution. As an undergraduate and master's-level student at San Diego State University, I received training in critical pedagogy. I then entered a doctoral program in sociology at the University of California, Santa Barbara, that included an emphasis on feminist studies and studies of race and ethnicity. This unique interdisciplinary training has shaped my research and overarching goals.

Abrams, L. S. (2000). Guardians of virtue: The social reformers and the "girl problem," 1890–1920. *Social Review* 74, 436–452.

Abrams, L. S., and Curran, L. (2000). Wayward girls and virtuous women: Social workers and female juvenile delinquency in the progressive era. *Affilia* 15, 49–64.

Alarid, L. F., Burton, J. V., and Cullen, F. T. (2000). Gender and crime among felony offenders: Assessing the generality of social control and differential association theories. *Journal of Research in Crime and Delinquency* 37 (2), 171–199.

Alexander, M. (2010). *The new jim crow: Mass incarceration in the age of colorblindness*. New York: New Press.

Anderson, E. (1999). *Code of the street: Decency, violence, and the moral life of the inner city*. New York: W. W. Norton.

Artz, S., and Nicholson, D. (2010). Negotiations of the living space: Life in the group home for girls who use violence. In M. Chesney-Lind and N. Jones, eds., *Fighting for girls: New perspectives on gender and violence* (pp. 149–174). Albany: State University of New York Press.

Barry, M. (2007). The transitional pathways of young female offenders: Towards a non-offending lifestyle. In R. Sheehan, G. McIvor, and C. Trotter, eds., *What works with women offenders*. Cullompton, U.K.: Willan Publishing.

Becker, H. (1953). Becoming a marihuana user. *American Journal of Sociology* 59 (3), 235–242.

Belknap, J. (2001). *The invisible women: Gender, crime and justice*. Belmont, CA: Wadsworth.

——— (2006). The gendered nature of risk factors for delinquency. *Feminist Criminology* 1 (1), 48–71.

Belknap, J., Holsinger, K., and Dunn, M. (1997). Understanding incarcerated girls: The results of a focus group study. *Prison Journal* 77 (4), 381–404.

Benda, B. (2005). Gender differences in life-course theory of recidivism: A survival analysis. *International Journal of Offender Therapy and Comparative Criminology* 49 (3), 325–342.

Bettie, J. (2003). *Women without class: Girls, race and identity.* Berkeley: University of California Press.

Bickel, C. (2010). From child to captive: Constructing captivity in a juvenile institution. *Western Criminology Review* 11 (1), 37–49.

Bloom, B., Owen, B., and Covington, S. (2004). Women offenders and the gendered effects of public policy. *Review of Policy Research* 21 (1), 31–47.

Bloom, B., Owen, B., Deschenes, E. P., and Rosenbaum, J. (2002). Moving toward justice for female juvenile offenders in the new millennium: Modeling gender specific policies and programs. *Journal of Contemporary Criminal Justice* 18 (1), 37–56.

Boyle, K., Polinsky, M. L., and Hser, Y. (2000). Resistance to drug abuse treatment: A comparison of drug users who accept or decline treatment referral assesment. *Journal of Drug Issues* 30, 555–574.

Bracy, N. (2010). Circumventing the law: Students' rights in schools with police. *Journal of Contemporary Criminal Justice* 26 (3), 294–315

Brown, M. (2010). Negotiations of the living space: Life in the group home for girls who use violence. In M. Chesney-Lind, and N. Jones, eds., *Fighting for girls: New perspectives on gender and violence* (pp. 175–199). Albany: State University of New York Press.

Burton-Rose, D. (2003). Our sisters' keepers. In T. Herivel and P. Wright, eds., *Prison nation: The warehousing of America's poor* (pp. 258–261). New York: Taylor and Francis.

California Department of Corrections and Rehabilitation. (1998). California State specifications: Youth correctional officer. September 1. www.cdcr.ca.gov /Career_Opportunities/POR/YCOIndex.html.

California Department of Education. (2012a). Community day schools. www .cde.ca.gov/sp/eo/cd/.

—— (2012b). Continuation education. www.cde.ca.gov/sp/eo/ce/.

—— (2012c). Continuation education—CalEdFacts. www.cde.ca.gov/sp/eo /ce/cefcontinuationed.asp.

—— (2015). Community Day Schools program summary. www.cde.ca.gov/sp /eo/cd/summarycds.asp.

California Legislative Analyst's Office (1995). Juvenile crime—outlook for California, part 5, www.lao.ca.gov/1995/050195_juv_crime/kkpart5.aspx.

—— (2007). California's criminal justice system: A primer. January 31. www .lao.ca.gov/2007/cj_primer/cj_primer_013107.aspx#Intro.

Cammarota, J. (2004). Latina and Latino youth: Different struggles, different resistances in the urban context. *Anthropology and Education Quarterly* 35 (1), 53–74.

Capaldi, L., Kim, H., and Owen, L. (2008). Romantic partners' influence on men's likelihood of arrest in early adulthood. *Criminology* 54 (1), 267–299.

Carbone-Lopez, K., and Miller, J. (2012). Precocious role entry as a mediating factor in women's methamphetamine use: Implications for life-course and pathways research. *Criminology* 50 (1), 187–220.

Casella, R. (2003). Punishing dangerousness through preventive detention: Illustrating the institutional link between school and prison. *New Directions for Youth Development* (99), 55–70.

Castro, F. G., Barrera, M., Jr., Pantin, H., Martinez, C., Felix-Ortiz, M., Rios, R., et al. (2006). Substance abuse prevention intervention research with Hispanic populations. *Drug and Alcohol Dependence*, 84S, S29–S42.

Champion, D. J. (2010). *The juvenile justice system: Delinquency, processing and the law.* New York: Pearson.

Chavez-Garcia, M. (2009). "The crime of precocious sexuality" celebrates thirty years: A critical appraisal. *Journal of the History of Childhood and Youth*, 2 (1), 88–94.

Chesney-Lind, M. (1986). Women and crime: The female offender. *Signs: Journal of Women in Culture and Society* 12 (1), 78–96.

—— (2006). Patriarchy, crime and injustice: Feminist criminology in an era of backlash. *Feminist Criminology* 1 (1), 6–26.

—— (2010). Jailing "bad" girls: Girls' violence and trends in female incarceration. In M. J. Chesney-Lind and N. Jones, eds., *Fighting for girls: New perspectives on gender and violence* (pp. 57–79). Albany: State University of New York Press.

Chesney-Lind, M., and Jones, N. (2010). *Fighting for girls: New perspectives on gender and violence.* Albany: State University of New York Press.

Chesney-Lind, M., and Pasko, L. (2004). *Girls, women and crime.* Thousand Oaks, CA: Sage.

—— (2012). *The female offender: Girls, women and crime.* Los Angeles: Sage.

Chesney-Lind, M., and Shelden, R. G. (2004). *Girls, delinquency, and juvenile justice.* 3rd ed. Belmont, CA: Wadsworth Cengage Learning.

Christle, C. A., Jolivette, K., and Nelson, C. M. (2005). Breaking the school to prison pipeline: Identifying school risk and protective factors for youth delinquency. *Exceptionality* 13 (2), 69–88.

Clemmer, D. (1940). *The prison community.* Boston: Christopher Publishing House.

Cole, H., and Heilig, J. (2006). Developing a school-based youth court: A potential alternative to the school to prison pipeline. *Journal of Law and Education* 40 (2), 305–322.

Collins, P. H. (2004). *Black sexual politics: African Americans, gender and new racism.* New York: Routledge.

Collins, R. (2008). *Violence: A micro-sociological theory.* Princeton, NJ: Princeton University Press.

Connell, R. W., and Messerschmidt, J. W. (2005). Hegemonic masculinity: Rethinking the concept. *Gender and Society* 19 (6), 829–859.

Crosland, K. A., Dunlap, G., Sager, W., Neff, B., Wilcox, C., Blanco, A., and Giddings, T. (2008). The effects of staff training on the types of interactions observed at two group homes for foster care children. *Research on Social Work Practice* 18 (5), 410–420.

Culbertson, R. (1975). The effects of institutionalization on the delinquent inmate's self-concept. *Journal of Criminal Law and Criminology* 66 (1), 88–93.

Dank, M. (2011). *The commercial sexual exploitation of children.* El Paso, TX: LFB Scholarly Publishing.

Darder, A. (2002). *Reinventing Paulo Freire: A pedagogy of love.* Boulder, CO: Westview Press.

Davis, A. (2003). *Are prisons obsolete?* New York: Seven Stories Press.

Dellasega, C., and Nixon, C. (2003). *Girl wars: 12 strategies that will end female bullying.* New York: Simon and Schuster.

De Velasco, J. R., Austin, G., Dixon, D., Johnson, J., McLaughlin, M., and Perez, L. (2008). Alternative education options: A descriptive study of California continuation high schools. In *National Center for Urban School Transformation issue brief.* Stanford, CA: John W. Gardner Center for Youth and Their Communities.

De Velasco, J. R., and McLaughlin, M. (2012). *Raising the bar, building capacity: Driving improvement in California's continuation schools.* Berkeley, CA: John W. Gardner Center for Youth and Their Communities.

Díaz-Cotto, J. (2006). *Chicana lives and criminal justice: Voices from el barrio.* Austin: University of Texas Press.

Dietrich, L. C. (1998). *Chicana adolescents: Bitches, 'ho's, and schoolgirls.* Westport: Praeger.

Duck, W. O. (2012). An ethnographic portrait of a precarious life: Gettting by on even less. *Annals of the American Academy of Political and Social Sciences* 642 (1), 124–138.

Dvoskin, J. A., and Spiers, E. M. (2004). On the role of correctional officers in prison mental health. *Psychiatric Quarterly* 75 (1), 41–49.

Elder, G. H. (1986). Military times and turning points in men's lives. *Developmental Psychology* 22, 233–245.

Elder, J. G. (1985). *Life course dynamics: Trajectories and transitions, 1968–1980.* Ithaca, NY: Cornell University Press.

Emerson, R. M., Fretz, R. I., and Shaw, L. L. (1995). *Writing ethnographic fieldnotes.* Chicago: University of Chicago Press.

Esterberg, K. G. (2002). *Qualitative methods in social research.* No. 300.18 E8. Boston: McGraw-Hill.

Fader, J. (2013). *Falling back: Incarceration and transitions to adulthood among urban youth.* New Brunswick, NJ: Rutgers University Press.

Farmer, S. (2010). Criminality of Black youth in inner-city schools: "Moral panic," moral imagination, and moral formation. *Race Ethnicity and Education* 13 (3), 367–381.

Feierman, M., Levick, M., and Mody, A. (2009). The school-to-prison pipeline . . . and back: Obstacles and remedies for the re-enrollment of adjudicated youth. *Education* 54, 1115–1130.

Finlay, L. (2002). "Outing" the researcher: The provenance, process, and practice of reflexivity. *Qualitative Health Research* 12 (4), 531–545.

Flores, J. (2012). Jail pedagogy: Liberatory education inside a California juvenile detention facility. *Journal of Education for Students Placed at Risk* 17 (4), 286–300.

—— (2013). "Staff here let you get down": The cultivation and co-optation of violence in a California juvenile detention center. *Signs: The Jounal of Women and Culture* 39 (1), 221–241.

Foucault, M. (1977). *Discipline and punish: The birth of the prison.* 2nd ed. New York: Vintage Books.

—— (1978). *The history of sexuality.* 1st American ed. New York: Pantheon.

Fox, L. (1983). Obedience and rebellion: Revision of Chicana myths of motherhood. *Women's Studies Quarterly* 6 (2), 20–22.

Freire, P. (1970). *Pedagogy of the oppressed.* New York: Continuum International.

Gaarder, E., and Belknap, J. (2002). Tenuous borders: Girls, transferred to adult court. *Criminology* 40 (1), 481–517.

Garcia, L. (2012). *Respect yourself, protect yourself: Latina girls and sexual identity.* New York: New York University Press.

Garland, D. (1990). *Punishment and modern society.* Oxford: University of Chicago Press.

Gelsthorpe, L., and Sharpe, G. (2006). Gender, youth crime and justice. *Youth Crime and Justice* (May), 7–61.

Gillmore, R. W. (2003). *Golden gulag: Prisons, surplus, crisis, and opposition in globalizing California.* Berkeley: University of California Press.

Giordano, P. C., Cernkovich, S. A., and Rudolph, J. L. (2002). Gender, crime and desistance: Toward a theory of cognitive transformations. *American Journal of Sociology* 107 (4), 900–1064.

Glueck, S., and Glueck, E. T. (1950). *Unraveling juvenile delinquency*. Harvard Law School studies in criminology. New York: Commonwealth Fund.

Goffman, A. (2009). On the run: Wanted men in a Philadelphia ghetto. *American Sociological Review* 74 (3), 339–335.

Goffman, E. (1961). *Asylums: Essays on the social situation of mental patients and other inmates*. Chicago: Aldine.

González-López, G. (2006). Epistemologies of the wound: Anzaldúan theories and sociological research on incest in Mexican society. *Human Architecture: Journal of the Sociology of Self-Knowledge,* 17–24.

Goodkind, S. (2009). "You may even be president of the United States one day"? Challenging commercialized feminism in programming for girls in juvenile justice. In L. M. Nybell, J. J. Shook, and J. L. Finn, eds., *Childhood, youth, and social work in transformation: Implications for policy and practice* (pp. 364–84). New York: Columbia University Press.

Goodkind, S., and Miller, D. L. (2006). A widening of the net of social control? "Gender specific" treatment for young women in the U.S. juvenile justice system. *Journal of Progressive Human Services* 17, 45–70.

Gover, A. (2004). Childhood sexual abuse, gender and depression among incarcerated youth. *International Journal of Offender Therapy and Comparative Criminology* 48 (6), 683–696.

Hagan, J., and Palloni, A. (1990a). Crimes as social events in the life course. *Criminology* 26, 87–100.

——— (1990b). The social reproduction of a criminal class in working-class London, circa 1950–1980. *American Journal of Sociology*, 96 (2), 265–299.

Haney, C. (2001). *The psychological impact of incarceration: Implications for post-prison adjustment*. U.S. Department of Health and Human Services. https://aspe.hhs.gov/basic-report/psychological-impact-incarceration-implications-post-prison-adjustment.

Hannah-Moffat, K. (2003). Getting women out: The limits of reintegration reform. *Criminal Justice Matters* 53, 44–65.

Haynie, D., Giordano, P., Manning, W., and Longmore, M. (2005). Adolescent romantic relationships and delinquency involvement. *Criminology* 43 (1), 655–673.

Hirschfield, P. (2009). Another way out: The impact of juvenile arrests on high school dropout. *Sociology of Education* 82 (4), 368–393.

Holtfreter, K., Reisig, M., and Morash, M. (2004). Poverty, state capital, and recidivism among women offenders. *Criminology and Public Policy* 3 (2), 181–216.

Horning, A. (2013). Peeling the onion: Domestically trafficked minors and other sex work involved youth. *Dialectical Anthropology* 37, 299-307.

Hurd, Clayton A. (2004). "Acting out" and being a "schoolboy": Performance in an ELD classroom. In Margaret A. Gibson, Patricia Gándara, and Jill Peterson Koyama, eds., *School connections: U.S. Mexican youth, peers, and school achievement* (pp. 63-85). New York: Teachers College Press.

James, J. (1996). *Resisting state violence: Radicalism, gender and race in U.S. Culture.* Minneapolis: University of Minnesota Press.

Jones, N. (2008). Working "the code": On girls, gender, and inner-city violence. *Australian and New Zealand Journal of Criminology* 41 (1), 63-83.

—— (2010). *Between good and ghetto: African American girls and inner-city violence.* New Brunswick, NJ: Rutgers University Press.

Kakar, S., Friedemann, M.-L., and Peck, L. (2002). Girls in detention: The results of focus group discussion, interviews and official records review. *Journal of Contemporary Criminal Justice* 18 (1), 57-73.

Katz, S. (1997). Presumed guilty: How schools criminalize Latino youth. *Social Justice* 24 (4), 77-95.

Kim, C. Y., Losen, D. J., and Hewitt, D. T. (2010). *The school-to-prison pipeline: Structuring legal reform.* New York: New York University Press.

Kreager, D. A., Matsueda, R. L., and Erosheva, E. A. (2010). Motherhood and criminal desistance in disadvantaged neighborhoods. *Criminology* 48 (1), 221-258.

Kupchik, A. (2009). Things are tough all over: Race, ethnicity, class and school discipline. *Punishment and Society* 11 (3), 291-317.

—— (2010). *Homeroom security: School discipline in an age of fear.* New York: New York University Press.

Kupers, T. (2005). Toxic masculinity as a barrier to mental health treatment in prison. *Journal of Clinical Psychology* 61 (6), 713-724.

Lopez, V., Jurik, N., and Gilliard-Matthews, S. (2009). Gender, sexuality, power and drug acquisition strategies among adolescent girls who use meth. *Feminist Criminology* 4 (3), 226-251.

Los Angeles County Department of Children and Family Services. (2009). Wraparound overview. www.lacdcfs.org/katieA/wraparound/index.html.

Malagon, C., and Alvarez, M. C. (2010). Chicanas who go to college: Former Chicana continuation high school students disrupting the educational achievement binary. *Harvard Education Review* 80 (2), 149-174.

Mc-Daniels-Wilson, J., and Belknap, J. (2008). The extensive sexual violation and sexual abuse histories of incarcerated women. *Violence Against Women* 14 (10), 1090-1127.

McGrew, K. (2008). *Education's prisoners: Schooling, the political economy and the prison industrial complex*. New York: Peter Lang.

Mclvor, G., Trotter, C., and Sheehan, R. (2009). Women, resettlement and desistance. *Probation Journal: The Journal of Community and Criminal Justice* 56 (4), 347–361.

Miller, J. (2008). Getting played: African American girls, urban inequality and gendered violence. New York: New York University Press.

Morris, E. (2007). "Ladies" or "loudies"?: Perceptions and experiences of Black girls in classrooms. *Youth and Society* 38 (4), 490–515.

Muñiz, A. (2015). *Police, power and the production of racial boundaries*. New Brunswick, NJ: Rutgers University Press.

NAACP Legal Defense and Educational Fund (2005). *Dismantling the school-to-prison pipeline*. New York: Legal Defense Fund.

Okamoto, S. (2002). The challenges of male practitioners working with female clients. *Child and Youth Care Forum* 31 (4), 269–281.

Owen, B. (1998). *In the mix: Struggle and survival in a women's prison*. Albany: State University of New York Press.

——— (2003). Differences with a distinction: Women offenders and criminal justice practice. In B. E. Bloom, ed., *Gendered justice* (pp. 25–43). Durham, NC: Carolina Academic Press.

Paik, L. (2011). *Discretionary justice: Looking inside a juvenile drug court*. New Brunswick, NJ: Rutgers University Press.

Park, S., Morash, M., and Stevens, T. (2010). Gender differences in predictors of assaultive behavior in late adolescence. *Youth Violence and Juvenile Justice* 8 (4), 314–331.

Pasko, L. (2008). The wayward girl revisited: Understanding the gendered nature of juvenile justice and delinquency. *Sociology Compass* 3, 821–836.

——— (2010). Damaged daughters: The history of girls' sexuality and the juvenile justice system. *Journal of Criminal Law and Criminology* 100 (3), 1099–1130.

Pollock, J. (2002). *Women, prison and crime*. Pacific Grove, CA: Brooks/Cole Publishing.

Price, P. (2009). When is a police officer an officer of the law?: The status of police officers in schools. *Journal of Criminal Law and Criminology* 99 (2), 541–570.

Prothrow-Stith, D. (1991). *Deadly consequences*. New York: HarperCollins.

Prothrow-Stith, D., and Spivak, H. R. (2005). *Sugar and spice and no longer nice: How we can stop girls' violence*. San Francisco: Josey-Bass Press.

Rasche, C. E. (2003). Cross-sex supervision of incarcerated women and the dynamics of staff sexual misconduct. In B. E. Bloom, ed., *Gendered justice* (pp. 141–172). Durham, NC: Carolina Academic Press.

Rios, V. (2006). The hyper-criminalization of Black and Latino male youth in the era of mass incarceration. *Souls: A Critical Journal of Black Politics, Culture and Society* 8 (2), 40–54.

—— (2011). *Punished: Policing the lives of Black and Latino boys.* New York: New York University Press.

Rios, V., and Galicia, M. (2013). "Smoking guns or smoke and mirrors?: Schools and the policing of Latino boys." *Association for Mexican American Educators Journal* 7 (3), 32–41.

Romero, M. (2001). State violence and the social and legal construction of Latino criminality: From el bandido to gang member. *Denver University Law Review* 78 (4), 1081–1118.

Rotermund, S. (2007). *Alternative education enrollment and dropouts in California high schools.* Santa Barbara: California Dropout Research Project.

Sampson, R. J., and Laub, J. H. (1990). Crime and deviance over the life course: The salience of adult social bonds. *American Sociological Review* 55 (5), 609–627.

—— (1992). Crime and deviance in the life course. *Annual Review of Sociology* 18, 63–84.

—— (1993). *Crime in the making.* Cambridge, MA: Harvard University Press.

—— (1997). A life-course theory of cumulative disadvantage and the stability of delinquency. *Developmental Theories of Crime and Delinquency* 7, 133–161.

Schaffner, L. (1998). Searching for connection: A new look at teenaged runaways. *Adolescence* 33 (131), 619–628.

—— (2006). *Girls in trouble with the law.* New Brunswick, NJ: Rutgers University Press.

Schippers, M. (2007). Recovering the feminine other: Masculinity, femininity, and gender hegemony. *Theory and Society* 36 (1), 85–102.

Segura, D. (1993). Chicanas and triple oppression in the labor force. In T. Cordova, N. E. Cantu, G. Cardenas, J. Garcia, and C. M. Sierra, eds., *Chicana voices: Intersections of class, race, and gender* (pp. 47–65). Albuquerque: University of New Mexico Press.

Shannon, K., Bright, V., Gibson, K., and Tyndall, M. W. (2007). Sexual and drug-related vulnerabilities for HIV infection among women engaged in survival sex work in Vancouver, Canada. *Canadian Journal of Public Health* 98 (6), 465–469.

Sharma, S. (2010). Contesting institutional discourse to create new possibilities for understanding lived experience: Life stories of young women in detention, rehabilitation, and education. *Race, Ethnicity and Education* 13 (3), 327–347.

Shelden, R. G. (2010). *Our punitive society: Race, class and punishment in America.* Long Grove, IL: Waveland Press.

Simkins, S. B., Hirsch, A. E., Horvat, E. M. and Moss, M. B (2004). The school to prison pipeline for girls: The role of physical and sexual abuse. *Children's Legal Rights Journal* 24 (4), 56–72.

Simons, R. L., Stewart, L. G., Conger, J. R., and Elder, G. (2002). Test of life-course explanations for stability and change in antisocial behavior from adolescence to young adulthood. *Criminology* 40 (2), 401-434.

Skyes, G. M. (1958). *The society of captives: A study of a maximum security prison.* Princeton, NJ: Princeton University Press.

Smith, J. P. (2003). Assimilation across the Latino generations. *American Economic Review* 93 (2), 315-319.

Soto, S. (1986). Tres modelos culturales: La virgen de guadelupe, la malinche y la llorona. *Fem* 10 (48), 13-16.

Steffensmeir, D. J. (1980). Sex differences in patterns of adult crime, 1965–77: A review and assesment. *Social Forces* 58 (4), 1080-1108.

Steffensmeier, D., Schwartz, J., Zhong, H., and Ackerman, J. (2005). An assessment of recent trends in girls' violence using diverse longitudinal sources: Is the gender gap closing? *Criminology* 43 (2), 355-406.

Tapia, R. (2010). Certain failures: Representing the experiences of incarcerated women in the United States. In R. Solinger, P. C. Johnson, M. L. Raimon, T. Reynolds, and R. Tapia, eds., *Interrupted life* (pp. 1-6). Berkeley: University of California Press.

Thomas, D., and Stevenson, H. (2009). Gender risks and education: The particular classroom challenges for urban low-income African American boys. *Review of Research in Education* 33 (1), 160–180.

Thornberry, T. P. (1997). *Developmental theories of crime and delinquency.* New Brunswick, NJ: Transaction Publishers.

Trujillo, K. A., Castaneda, E., Martinez, D., and Gonzalez, G. (2006). Biological research on drug abuse and addiction in Hispanics: Current status and future directions. *Drug and Alcohol Dependence* 84S, S17–S28.

U.S. Department of Justice (2003). *Triple C fact sheet: Questions and answers.* Washington, DC: National Drug Intelligence Center.

—— (2009). *Juvenile residential facility census, 2004: Selected findings.* Washington, DC: Office of Juvenile Justice and Delinquency Prevention.

Van Brunschot, E., and Brannigan, A. (2002). Childhood maltreatment and subsequent conduct disorder: The case of female street prostitution. *International Journal of Law and Psychiatry* 25 (3), 219-234.

Vanderbeck, R. M. (2005). Masculinity and fieldwork: Widening the discussion. *Gender, Place and Culture* 12 (4), 387-402.

Vigil, D. J. (2008). Female gang members from East Los Angeles. *International Journal of Social Inquiry* 1 (1), 47-74.

Wacquant, L. (2002). The curious eclipse of prison ethnography in the age of mass incarceration. *Ethnography* 3 (4), 371-397.

Wald, J., and Losen, D. (2003). Defining and redirecting a school-to-prison pipeline. *New Directions for Youth development* (99), 9-15.

Warner, L. A., Valdez, A., Vega, W. A., de la Rosa, M., Turner, R. J., and Canino, G. (2006). Hispanic drug abuse in an evolving cultural context: An agenda for research. *Drug and Alcohol Dependence* 84, S8-S16.

Winn, M. (2010). "Our side of the story": Moving incarcerated youth voices from margins to center. *Race, Ethnicity and Education* 13 (3), 313-325.

—— (2011). *Girl time: Literacy, justice and the school-to-prison pipeline.* New York: Teachers College Press.

Wyse, J., Harding, D., and Morenoff, J. (2014). Romantic relationships and criminal desistance: Pathways and processes. *Sociological Forum* 29 (2), 365-385.

Zabel, R., and Nigro, F. (2007). Occupational interests and aptitudes of juvenile offenders: Influence of special education experience and gender. *Journal of Correctional Education*, 337-355.

Zanis, D., Mulvaney, F., and Coviello, D. (2003). The effectiveness of early parole to substance abuse treatment facilities. *Journal of Drug Issues* 33 (1), 223-235.

Zavella, P. (1993). "Feminist insider dilemmas: Constructing ethnic identity with Chicana informants. *Frontiers: A Journal of Women Studies* 13 (3), 53-76.

hierarchies, 10; and power hierarchies, 10; and return to Legacy, 6;
treatment at, 6; and wraparound
services, 136
De Velasco, J. R., 81
deviance, 12–14, 112–13, 116–17
Díaz-Cotto, J., 8
disabilities, learning, 17, 21, 99–100
disrespect/respect, 52, 61–62; by
correctional staff, 69, 132; and
fighting, 55, 57–58; and violence
strategy, 52
domestic abuse, 30–31, 41, 42, 114, 131
drug abuse, 111–12; author's personal
experiences of, 145; beginning of,
38–40; drug addictions, 31, 38–41,
42, 132, 135; drug rehabilitation, 112;
and friends, 167Ch1n2; by parents,
32–33; and participants, 28; and
Recuperation Program, 23; risk of,
150; and turning points, 14. *See also*
drug use; substance abuse
drug testing, 5, 22, 72, 118, 135
drug use: and dating, 40–41, 111; and
families, 38, 39–40, 41–42; and first
arrest, 47, 112; and targeting, 136. *See
also* drug abuse
Duck, W. O., 36

economic factors: and criminal justice
system, 6, 112, 139, 140–41; poverty,
11, 12, 15, 28–29, 36, 37, 150; and
public education connection, 6,
18, 139. *See also* socioeconomic
factors
educational system: academic factors,
17, 134; academic rule violations,
136–37; academic sanctions, 72;
administration, 22, 108, 115, 136,
166n8; compulsory education laws,
145; dropouts, 145; graduation, 110,
114–15, 118, 120, 128–29; higher
education, 112, 118, 124; and penal
system connection, 7, 72, 138; and
successful transitions, 14; surveillance of, 130; suspensions, 22, 27, 90,
136

educators: and educational methods,
166n5; and institutional harassment,
136; positive interventions, 27;
teaching methods, 57–58, 166n5; use
of fighting, 57–58
electronic monitoring, 48–49, 131; and
traditional school mistreatment, 136
El Valle Juvenile Detention Facility: daily
schedule in, 53–54; demographic
information, 20–21; description of,
2–5, 93; effects of first incarceration
in, 131; and Legacy Community
School, 7, 139; and Legacy Community School connection, 22;
negotiating life in, 132; overview of,
20–21; Probation Department, 23;
Recuperation Program, 22–23,
134–35; and violence participation,
52, 133
Emerson, R. M., 25
Emma (participant), 143
employment, 118, 122–23, 124; achievement of, 112; lack of, 28, 122–23, 124;
leading to successful transitions, 14;
and social bonds, 112, 117; and youth
control complex, 165n4
Erosheva, E. A., 111
ethnic factors. *See* racial factors
Eve (participant), 162tab.1
exploitation, 150
expulsions, 18, 27, 91, 107, 109, 116, 136

Fader, J., 13
families: and desistance, 111; and drug
use, 38, 39–40, 41–42; and intergenerational ties to gangs, 123; sexual
abuse from, 29–30; and social bonds,
112, 117; and youth control complex,
165n4
Feliz (participant), 32–34, 41–42, 55–56,
59–61, 67, 69, 107–8, 110, 114–16, 121,
155–57, 162tab.1, 164tab.1
feminist criminology, 29, 111, 112–13, 138,
139
fighting/fighters: avoidance of, 62 69;
correctional staff use of reputations,
56–59; decisions regarding, 59–61;

formal probation, 73; as wraparound incarceration, 71–72
reflexivity, 144–46
rehabilitation, 11, 72
reintegration, 27, 136
relational isolation, 64, 133
Rene (participant), 163tab.1
replacement self, 14
reputations, 56, 61–64
research process, 143–160; challenges of, 144, 153; data collection methods, 24–26; ethnographic research methods, 24–26; fieldwork issues, 153–56; gaining access to El Valle facility, 146–47, 158; and healthy boundaries, 156–59; and hegemonic masculinity, 150–51; human-subject review process, 148; and hypersexualization behaviors, 150–51, 153–55, 158–59; and inappropriate behavior reports, 155–56; privilege, acknowledgment of in, 152–53; and reflexivity, 144–46; triangulation approach, 25; trust issues, 153; and victimization, 151
respect/disrespect, 61–62; by correctional staff, 69, 132; and fighting, 55, 57–58; and violence strategy, 52
Rios, V., 140, 165n4
romantic partners: and criminal justice system, 111–12; and domestic violence, 111–12, 131; and drug use, 38, 40–41, 111–12; effects on home life, 32–37, 120; and exiting criminal justice system, 111, 126–27; and runaways, 43–44, 125–26. See also sexuality factors
Rudolph, J. L., 13, 124, 139
runaways, 43, 86–88, 125–26. See street living

safety: and criminal justice system, 112; isolation choice, 133; relational isolation, 64; and violence strategy, 26, 52, 64, 132–33, 140
Sammy (participant), 163tab.1
Sampson, R. J., 12–13

Sanchez, Ms (teacher), 28, 57–58, 115
Sandra (participant), 40–41, 47, 64, 93–94, 96, 163tab.1, 164tab.1
Sandy (teaching aid), 68
Sarah (participant), 163tab.1
Schaffner, L., 150
Schippers, M., 151
school pathways, 7
schools: and academic/criminal sanctions, 72; connection to institutions of confinement, 7, 130; and first arrest, 47–48; harassment in, 103–9; institutionalization, 93–109; and return to Legacy, 6; school/detention link, 130; school resource officers, 15–16; and security officers, 72; and social bonds, 112, 117; treatment at, 6; and youth control complex, 165n4. See also alternative education; educational system; traditional school
school-to-prison pipeline, 138, 145
secure detention, 52, 136
segregation, 18, 20, 22, 28
sexual abuse: in the community, 29; in correctional facilities, 147; experiences of, 8; in the home, 29, 119; of incarcerated women, 149; incarceration link, 149; and race, class, gender and sexuality, 131; and street living, 45–47
sexuality factors: and continuation schools, 17; and criminalization, 10, 150; of experiences, 7; hypersexualization, 17–18, 150; influencing experience at school, 17; premarital sex, 11; and punishment, 27, 152; sexual harassment, 17, 167Ch3n3; sexualized behaviors, 144; sexually transmitted disease, 150; sexual mistreatment risks, 150; sex work, 45–47; shaping incarceration experiences, 11, 28; shaping pathways, 7. See also romantic partners
Shannon (participant), 66, 163tab.1, 164tab.1

CPSIA information can be obtained
at www.ICGtesting.com
Printed in the USA
LVHW03s2248260618
582006LV00005B/8/P